Uncle Tom Cobley and All

Printed music sheet page of 'Widdicombe Fair', 1889.

Uncle Tom Cobley and All

The history of 'Widdicombe Fair'

Todd Gray

THE MINT PRESS

2019

To the memory of Tony Beard,
friend & colleague

First published 2019

Cover illustration: 'Widdicombe Fair' by Stanley Baker, 1912 (private collection)
Title page illustration: *A fair in the country*, by Thomas Rowlandson, no date

ISBN 978 1 903356 73 9

The Mint Press, Taddyforde House South, Taddyforde Estate,
New North Road, Exeter EX4 4AT

Distribution through Stevensbooks: www.stevensbooks.co.uk
sales@themintpress.co.uk
01392 459760

Printed and bound in Great Britain by Short Run Press Ltd, Exeter

Contents

Appendices: The Song

Contents

Foreword

My interest in Tom Cobley began in 1995 when I happened upon an unknown version of 'Widdicombe Fair'. I realised then that these lyrics were much earlier than those which Sabine Baring-Gould had made famous in 1889 and that they were also very different. I made a note to return to it once I had some free time. Twenty-two years later I rediscovered that note.

During this interval my own research interests had broadened from the period between the Reformation and the Civil War to becoming more interested in Devon as a whole. I have also become aware that since the mid 1990s popular interest in the history of Devon has gradually narrowed to that in the sub-regions of the South Hams, East Devon, West Devon, Dartmoor, North Devon, Exeter and Plymouth. The study of the ballad is a timely reminder of the importance of looking at the whole of the county let alone of placing it in a much wider context. Also, during this interval Martin Graebe had comprehensively written the background to song collecting in Victorian Devon. Two years ago I planned on limiting my contribution to writing a short note on this 'new' version. However, not long into the research, as dozens of other variants came to light, it became apparent that the ballad itself required a more in-depth treatment. To date 'Widdicombe Fair' has received only a passing consideration despite it having achieved worldwide fame. Devon has made few other cultural contributions which have had such an overwhelming and yet unassuming impact. 'My' unknown version was only a part, albeit an important one, of a much more interesting and yet still untold story. The aim of the project formed itself: to not only investigate the variant but also to redefine this iconic part of Devon's heritage.

The history of 'Widdicombe Fair' has proved to be wide-ranging and has necessitated the help of a number of friends and colleagues. Gabriella & Hugh Bullock, Roger Cooper, Lady Violet de Vere, Jill Drysdale, Dr Tom Greeves, John Heal, Carole Herbert, Phil Keen, Bob Mann, Stanley Oldfield, Dr Caroline Philpott, Dr Tim Rees, Tom Sawford, Geoffrey Sparkes and Professor Andrew Thorpe have been helpful in many different ways including generously responding to disparate and often singular questions. Andy Blunden was instrumental in deciphering Karl Marx's Cobley connection and Dr Lawrence Normand cheerfully investigated resources at the British Library. Professor Richard Hitchcock and Keith Stevens provided translations for two of the variants. Alan Rosevear has been helpful since the start of the project and I am particularly grateful to him for his enthusiasm and encouragement. He has also drawn the county map and along with Martin Graebe, Sue Jackson and Dr Andrew Thrush has considerably improved the text. Any and all mistakes remain, of course, my own.

I would also like to acknowledge help given by the staff of the Embassy of Argentina in London, Devon & Exeter Institution, Devon Heritage Centre, North Devon Record Office, and Unilever Art, Archives & Records Management as well as Sean Vis (BBC Written Archives Centre), Dr Janet Topp Fargion & Neil Raj (British Library), Rosie Woolson (Guinness Archive), Kaitlyn Crain Enriquez (National Archives & Record Administration), Anne Knight (Old Cornwall Society), Angela Broome (Royal Institution of Cornwall), Caroline Marchant-Wallis (Special Collections, University of East Sussex), Niki Russell (Special Collections, University of Glasgow), John McCrory (Special Collections, University of Manchester), Mary Sackett (Special Collections, University of Sheffield), Nick Wall (Vaughan Williams Memorial Library) and Uncle Tom Cobley and All. Version 45 is reproduced with the permission of Miles Fenton and Version 49 appears courtesy of the University of Manchester Library.

Taddyforde, Exeter
August 2019

The excursionists resting in the churchyard, by Pamela Colman Smith, 1898.

Map of Devon showing those places particularly associated with 'Widecombe Fair'.

ONE

The triumph of 'Widdicombe Fair'

When 'Widdicombe Fair' was first published in 1889 the expedition of Tom Cobley, his companions and an unnamed grey horse was drawn out of the public house and into concert halls and drawing rooms across the country. It became Devon's unofficial anthem though earlier that year another version had been printed which had failed to capture the public's imagination. A reviewer in St Albans summarised the appeal of 'Widdicombe Fair' as an 'old Devonshire song' which told 'the strange doings of Tom Pearce's mare and its numerous attendants'. The public embraced the ballad with enthusiasm, partly because it had a peculiar story but also because audiences were so delighted with the chorus that they inevitably joined in.[1] 'Widdicombe Fair' achieved the distinction of becoming Devon's most familiar song to audiences far beyond the West Country: in St Albans in 1950 William Brewer complained in court that boys were taunting him by repeatedly singing the chorus 'With Bill Brewer and Jan Stewer…'[2]

The ballad has had some odd incarnations: it was rewritten at Blundell's School in 1904 to teach 'the new mathematical system of approximation and the metric system of weights and measures'; Fleetwood Mac have repeatedly thanked Uncle Tom Cobley and All for help producing the band's albums; Cobley has even featured in the *Adventures of TinTin*.[3]

As if these were not odd bedfellows, Cobley was mentioned in the trial of Liberal Party Leader Jeremy Thorpe in 1979 and an English music hall star adapted the lyrics in the 1940s to help her prepare for her American citizenship test. Her version was:

George Washington, George Washington, lend me thy grey mare
    All along, out along, down along lea
I want for to go to Widdicombe Fair
    With John Adams, Thomas Jefferson, James Madison,
James Monroe, John Quincy Adams, Andrew Jackson,
    Old Martin Van Buren and all.[4]

More recently, IBM trained computer programmers by including the mare's excursionists in 'a subroutine to simplify tabulation'. The men were given occupations:

Call tabout Bill, Brewer, innkeeper
'Call tabout Jan, Stewer, cook
'Call tabout Peter, Gurney, farmer
'Call tabout Peter, Davey, labourer
'Call tabout Daniel, Whiddon, gamekeeper
'Call tabout Harry, Hawke, exciseman
'Call tabout Tom, Cobley, sailor (retired)[5]

Two separate court proceedings in Devon show how the ballad became embedded in local culture. In 1924, when six men were being prosecuted in Appledore, a journalist reported that their lawyer listed the men and then informed the jury that they:

Did not include Uncle Tom Cobley and all.
His Lordship (puzzled): Who? (laughter)
Mr Hancock: Uncle Tom Cobley and all (laughter)
His Lordship: Uncle Tom what? (laughter)
Mr Hancock: I think the jury will appreciate that it is a local touch.
His Lordship: What's his full name?
Mr Hancock: Uncle Tom Cobley. He is well known in these parts.
His Lordship: Oh! (laughter)[6]

In 1964 the song was again brought up in a Devon court. Five men were driving from Plymouth to Tavistock when two of the car's tyres fell off. The car was abandoned and during the subsequent legal proceedings the solicitor told magistrates the only precedent he knew was Tom Pearce's old mare. It was suggested:

First of four watercolours by Stanley Baker, 1912, illustrating the tale of the grey mare. Twelve excursionists ride in a wagon to the fair and recklessly return.

All along, down along, went John Jones' car
When two wheels came off, it couldn't go far
John Jones and his men had a hair-raising ride
And then the old car, her took sick and died.[7]

During the last years of the nineteenth century 'Widdicombe Fair' not only permeated Devonian culture but that of the nation. It was because of the song that the man who had broken the news of the discovery of Tutankhamun's tomb made a pilgrimage to Widecombe. He wrote:

How many times, and in how many lands, I have assisted in the journey of
Tom Pearce's grey mare to Widecombe I cannot say. I suppose that in every
part of the world in which Englishmen retain their voices, and particularly
wherever there is a Devonian, this old grey mare of Tom Pearce's has jogged
along to the tinkle of wineglasses with Bill Brewer, Jan Stewer, Peter Gurney,
Peter Davey, Dan'l Whiddon, Harry Hawke, old Uncle Tom Cobleigh and all![8]

Moreover, varieties of potatoes and heather have been named Tom Cobley. Other varieties of heather have been named Daniel Whiddon, Harry Hawke, Tom Pearce, Peter Gurney and Jan Stewer, all of whom feature in the ballad. Just as intriguingly, the grey mare was grown in topiary in Cornwall; the village of Widecombe-in-the-Moor was recreated in Sussex and Kent for charity fundraising; and Princess Marina, later known as HRH the Duchess of Kent, danced to the ballad as a foxtrot.[9]

The journey of Tom Pearce's mare to Widecombe Fair, her subsequent death and the naming of all the excursionists became as familiar as the final figure in the drama: the very name Tom Cobley has lent itself to a phrase which remains in common usage. Also, it will be shown how there have always been many versions of the song: recently a writer casually observed that Homer, Ovid and Uncle Tom Cobley were similar in that each has variations.[10] This surprising linking of three very different men is part of an unsuspecting history of the ballad which has until now gone unwritten. The chance discovery of a variant sung in Feniton in 1867 as well as a parody two years later written in Dartmouth, together with the bringing together of dozens of other versions for this study, helps to draw out this unknown history.

Public response to the ballad's publication

The ballad was propelled into fame by Sabine Baring-Gould's decision to include it in his *Songs and Ballads of the West; Folk Songs Collected From The Mouths Of The People*. Baring-Gould was the vicar of Lew Trenchard and had written numerous books as well as 'Onward Christian Soldiers'. In 1899 he reinvented 'Widdicombe Fair' by rewriting the lyrics, reducing the number of verses and devising a title with its unusual spelling of Widecombe.[11] One book reviewer commented:

> Several of the ballads will be recognised by persons who have spent any considerable time among the country folk of Dartmoor and its borders. One or two of them, such as *Widdecombe Fair* with its rollicking chorus of Uncle Tom Cobley and All, we have ourselves heard sung time after time in the capital of the county.[12]

Baring-Gould began a promotional tour in Exeter which took in South Brent, Tavistock, Plymouth, Newton Abbot, Torquay, Totnes, Sidmouth, Exmouth, Dawlish, Barnstaple, Bideford and Tiverton before extending to Cornwall, Bristol and then finally London. It was advertised as a 'Costume Concert Lecture': Baring-Gould was accompanied by a troupe of singers. One reviewer thought it was 'the most instructive and delightful entertainment ever taken through the county'. The tour lasted two years during which time the singers changed. Baring-Gould himself was unable to lecture in every location; in Bideford, for example, 'a worthy gentleman in a blue velvet suit, ruffles and silken hose' replaced him. The concerts were so popular that hundreds of Plymothians were turned away on one evening. The tour reached its zenith at Torquay with a performance, by request, in the presence of HRH Princess Louise.[13] Even so, towards the end of his life Baring-Gould admitted to feeling disappointed by the lacklustre response of professional musicians.[14]

The notices of 'Widdicombe Fair' were enthusiastic. Reviewers wrote it 'created much merriment', 'was re-demanded and the latter verses repeated' and it 'carried the house by storm'.[15] It was quickly included in other singers' performances not only throughout the West Country but also across England in such places as Windsor, Ambleside, Beccles, Eythorne (Kent), Reading, Cambridge and Chippenham.[16] The reports' use of the archaic spelling of Widdicombe demonstrates the song was spread by publication in *Songs of the West*.

Tom Pearce in despair upon finding the mare amidst the wreckage and bodies which are surrounded by ghosts.

The tale is told in a public house.

The ballad has periodically made appearances at Westminster. In 1920 the Minister for Labour sang 'Widdicombe Fair' to a roomful of disabled servicemen in London, ten years later a Plymouth MP referred to Cobley in Parliament and in 1967 his name was again resurrected during a House of Commons debate on the bombing of North Vietnam. In a later debate Lord Jacques asked 'Who was this Uncle Tom Cobley?'[17]

The appeal of Baring-Gould's ballad was universal but it found its initial response in Devonian public gatherings in the 1890s and early 1900s such as at the Venison Feasts of the Stag Hunt on Exmoor. American Scouts from Pennsylvania in 1927 were introduced to it at Two Bridges on Dartmoor. Their leader recorded 'It was the first time we had heard the ballad and it is a dandy. Everywhere in Devon they sing it.'[18]

However, from the start Devonians were unsure of the song's origins even as they embraced it. In 1897 one writer was confident it had begun in Devon but believed it was unfamiliar outside Dartmoor. Whereas one commentator asserted that in the 1880s it had been unknown in Ashburton another recalled having heard it in Exeter.[19] In 1928 a Dartmoor guidebook noted with confidence that 'Widdicombe Fair' 'is and always will be the Song of the Moor, and can almost claim to be the county anthem.'[20] Others went further. At a musical event in Somerset in 1901 the song was introduced as 'the Devonshire National Anthem' and this same sentiment was again expressed in 1932 'Pioneers from the West Country have carried to the ends of the earth the words and tunes of Devon's national anthem.'[21]

Another commented:

> It is a capital tune with a good refrain and has been adopted by Devonshire
> men as a sort of county anthem. But as to whether it is a genuine Devonshire
> song – that is quite another matter.[22]

Nevertheless, many Devonians considered the song as their own. In 1905 a Sussex writer associated Devon with cider, junket, clotted cream and 'Widdicombe Fair'.[23] A few years earlier a Torquay columnist had a public spat with a reader regarding his credentials as a Devonian: the journalist asserted that no one could call himself a Devonian who did not know 'Widdicombe Fair'. He wrote:

> I am very sorry for him, that is all. Did not the Rev. J. Baring-Gould make
> the song popular throughout the country with his lectures on West Country
> ballads? Do not the Haytors today gallantly march to its strains? Is it not sung

First of two pages of illustrations by Thomas Cantrell Dugdale, 1906.

NOVEMBER 24, 1906]   THE SPHERE   23

Then Tom Pierce's old mare her took zick an' died
All along out along down along lea...
An' Tom Pierce he zat down on a stone an' he cried
Wi' Bill Brewer, Jan Stewer, Peter Gurney,
Peter Davey, Dan'l Whiddon, Harry Hawke,
Old Uncle Tom Cobley and all,
Old Uncle Tom Cobley and all.

When the wind whustles cold on the moor of a night
All along out along down along lea..........
Tom Pierce's old mare doth appear, gashly white
Wi' Bill Brewer, Jan Stewer, Peter Gurney, Peter
Davey, Dan'l Whiddon, Harry Hawke, Old Uncle
Tom Cobley and all, Old Uncle Tom Cobley and all.

An' all the night long be heard skirling and groans
All along out along down along lea......
From Tom Pierce's old mare and her rattling bones
An' Bill Brewer, Jan Stewer, Peter Gurney, Peter Davey,
Dan'l Whiddon, Harry Hawke, Old Uncle Tom Cobley
and all, Old Uncle Tom Cobley and all

at all gatherings where Devonshire men are?... Whoever you are, teach it not only to yourself, but to those other London Devonians who know nothing of its beauty, its pathos, and tragedy. No, I certainly do not hold that you and they must be spurious – unfortunately I was not present at your birth and you were, so that you ought to know – but it certainly has come as a revelation to me that anyone born in the finest county in the world, could be ignorant of dear old 'Widdicombe Fair'.

I wonder... if you know clotted cream when you see it, or have probed into the inner mysteries of *wort* pie? Surely your education has been vastly neglected? It is really as bad as a Highlander being unable to dance a sword dance, or an Irishman unable under any provocation to wield a shillelagh? I hope that I have aroused in your breast a spirit of patriotism, a feeling of unquenchable loyalty to your county, which will not be appeased until you have learned words, music, and all of the old ballad of 'Widdicombe Fair'.[24]

Performances

The ballad was spread through a great number of public performances by a surprising range of singers. For instance, it was in the repertoire of the 'Cockney Song Scholars', a group of boys who were 'rescued' from the slums of London. A tour of England in 1936 included a performance of 'Widdicombe Fair' in the village itself. Twenty-four years previously, in 1910, it had been highly popular at the Westcountry Festival in London; one man commented 'wherever you went you heard... verses of Widdicombe Fair'.[25]

It was constantly performed by Devonians, including the Devonshire Regiment which used it as a marching song in South Africa,[26] and Devon sailors sung it overseas in Hong Kong and Shanghai.[27] The ballad was played as far afield as New Zealand in 1898 and fifty years later it was the most popular piece in one performer's repertoire during her 50,000 mile Australian tour. It was claimed 'no item has made such appeal to the Australian public'.[28]

Some of the worldwide renditions are intriguing. For example, an Englishman in the early 1900s chose it as his party piece to entertain French Legionnaires in the Sahara, it has been sung by men climbing Mount Everest, by a walker in a trek across Asia Minor during the Great War and in the early 1930s a gold prospector in Australia sung it in between shooting dingoes and searching for gold.[29] The Edwardian explorers of the Antarctic had one of the most fascinating renderings: they adapted it as a 'sledging song' for use across the ice and snow. (Version 46)

The ballad found eager audiences during the Great War including in a Wiltshire army camp[30] and with men convalescing at the Duke of Westminster's home in Cheshire. A performing soldier recalled:

> I remember that in one of our concerted numbers, Old Uncle Tom Cobley and
> All, I introduced several new characters into the list of names in the refrain,
> including the Duke of Westminster, which apparently amused them very much.

It featured in a Red Cross concert in Hammersmith at which the performers wore clothing 'after the fashion of land girls'.[31]

It was often sung to men serving overseas during the war. This included a group of soldiers stationed in France who were entertained in what was described as 'one of those rough-and-ready theatres in which soldiers nightly perform to soldiers behind the front'. An observer approved of their abilities and thought 'the grey mare dies in the most approved fashion and reappears in a realistic storm as a truly satisfying ghost'. Soldiers in India heard 'The Devon Dumplings' sing the ballad but English prisoners of war in a Turkish camp in Baghdad were less fortunate. They were prevented from finishing 'Widdicombe Fair' because their captives thought it was a Russian song denigrating Turkey.[32] That same year other English soldiers, stationed 'somewhere in France' a few miles behind the Front Line, transported a borrowed piano in a handbarrow to a barn where they sang the ballad to their comrades. The performers proved, according to one observer, that 'they were as good at singing as fighting, which is saying a great deal'. It was also the choice of George Mallory, the celebrated climber, during Christmas at the end of the war. He performed a parody for his men based on the life of a gun crew.[33]

Performances continued in the Second World War including one by Joyce Grenfell who sang to troops in Damascus. It was also during that war that Sir Patrick Leigh Fermor translated the ballad into Italian in order to entertain members of the Greek Resistance on Crete. Likewise, it was while on-board a navy vessel off the Azores that Graham Greene heard members of the Fleet Air Arm sing it one Christmas Eve.[34] During the war four of the mare's company publicly endorsed the war effort: a local authority fire prevention form listed local firewatchers as 'Brewer, William; Stewer, James; Gurney, Peter; Hawke, Harry'.[35]

'Widdicombe Fair' was widely introduced to North America through a tour of the 'Songs of the West' company in 1899. Performances in private homes, at home or abroad, were far less likely to be recorded. An unusual one which was noted involved Beatrice Webb, the social reformer. Charles Robert Ashbee, the leading Arts & Crafts proponent sang 'Widdicombe Fair' to her with the first line 'Mrs Webb, will you lend me your grey mare?'[36]

Recordings

An early composition was played in Dartmouth in 1865 when gentlemen and ladies attending the assembly danced to 'Uncle Tom's Cobley's Quadrille'. This was the composition of Stephen Jarvis, a local conductor who was otherwise described as a music professor and was employed as the Singing Master at the Middle-Class Public School.[37] His work does not appear to have survived but many of the ballad's other diverse musical arrangements and adaptions have survived and some in their original recordings. In 1915 Julius Harrison wrote an orchestral composition ('Humoresque Quartet for Strings') and when performed that year by the London String Quartet one reviewer commented it was 'an amusing trifle that was all too short'. It was recorded in 1927. Nearly a century later the Chamber Ensemble of London recorded 'Variations on Widecombe Fair in the style of Paganini' and the 1st Battalion the Devon & Dorset Regiment included the ballad in its *Music from the Presentation of Colours*.[38]

In 1958 the Trinidadian pianist Winnifred Atwell played 'Widdicombe Fair' as part of her 38 minute *Around the World in 80 tunes*. In 1938 Leonard Feather and Ye Olde English Swynge Band featured Dave Wilkins singing a jazz version which had one verse:

Tom Pearce, Tom Pearce
He called me at dawn
For two jam sessions
I'm going to town
And when I get there I am going to blow on my horn with Louis Armstrong,
    Fats Waller, Benny Goodman, Benny Carter, Duke Ellington, Teddy Wilson,
        old Uncle Tom Dorsey and all
Old Uncle Tom Dorsey and All.[39]

In 1930 the Regal Dramatic Players not only sang but also preambled and interspersed 'Widdicombe Fair' with comic dialogue in indeterminate accents. There were conversations at the fair ('Look! There's the tattoo lady, let's go in. I'd like to see the pictures on her back. So would us all') and strong words from Mrs Pearce ('What did I tell you Tom Pearce? Letting those scrim-shanking, rum frugalers have the old mare. You ought to be ashamed of yourself. Out of this house, Tom Pearce, and look for her. And if you dare to come back without finding her, I'll give you a good walloping'). Some of Britain's top recording stars sang a version two years later and substituted their own names in the chorus including Binnie Hale, Harry Tate, Raymond Newell, Len Fillis, Albert Sandler, Stanley Holloway and Flotsam and Jetsam. Two well-known American folksingers, Burl Ives and Jimmie Rodgers, made recordings in 1941 and 1961. The latter introduced the song by explaining that Tom Pearce 'was a very nice guy who would give his friends the shirt off his back' while the former enlightened listeners by telling them:

> There was a lot of fog around there and at that time a lot of wild horses. So if
> a wild horse would run through the night, the people used to believe that it
> was the ghost of Tam Pearce's old grey mare with the ghosts of all these men
> riding astride it.

In the late 1960s the ballad attracted contemporary musicians such as Renaissance, an English progressive rock band, and before them The Nashville Teens, an English rock band. Of the latter group Ray Phillips recalls that 'Widdicombe Fair' was his choice; he had liked folk music since his early teen years. Phillips suggested the song to the rest of the band who felt they could adapt it to fit their sound.[40]

At this time it was also sung by The George Mitchell Minstrels, by Jon Pertwee in a voice similar to his later incarnation Worzel Gummidge and by the King's Singers, a cappella vocal ensemble. More recently it has been taken up by the Ionian Singers, a chamber choir, by Show of Hands, an acoustic roots/folk duo, and by Professor Arthur C. Throovest in one of the most original renditions.[41]

In print, on stage and film

It was a favourite song of literary men such as D. H. Lawrence, Robert Graves, Robert Louis Stevenson and the poet Edward Thomas but this was part of a much more

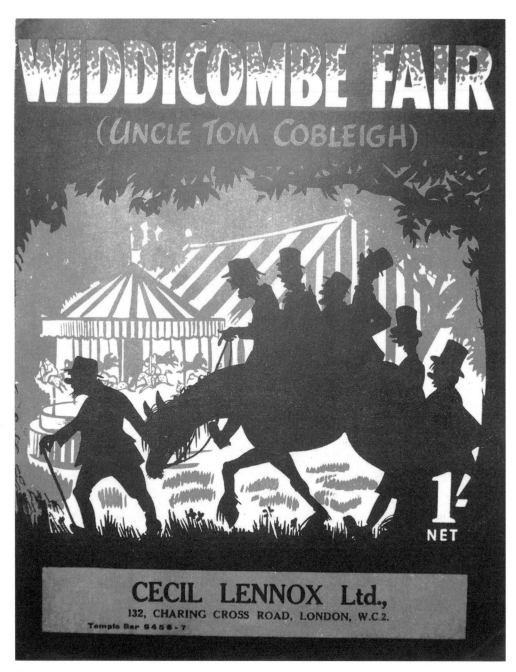

Sheet music for 'Widdicombe Fair', 1947.

Sheet music for 'Uncle Tom Cobleigh', 1920.

extensive literary presence.[42] It has been included in anthologies such as *Popular British Ballads* (1894), *British Songs for British Boys* (1903), *A Book of British Ballads* (1912), *One Hundred Songs of England* (1914), *Folk-Songs, Chanteys and Singing Games* (1916), *The Oxford Book of Ballads* (1920), *The Oxford Song Book* (1921), *The Way of Poetry* (1922), *Come Hither* (1923), *The Week-end Book* (1926), *The Celtic Song Book* (1928), *The Poets Highway Book* (1929), *The Queen's Treasures Book of Verse* (1932), *Poems for Youth* (1935), *Verse Worth Remembering* (1940), *Freedom Songs of the United Nations* (1943), *Fireside Book of Folk Songs* (1947), *A Treasury of Folk Songs* (1948), *Les grands lyriques anglais* (1948), *An Inheritance of Poetry* (1948), *Penguin Song Book* (1951), *The Boy's Book of Verse* (1951), *One Hundred Story Poems* (1951), *The Moon is Shining Bright as Day* (1953), *The Merry-Go-Round* (1955), *The New National and Folk Song Book* (1958*), Ducks and Dragons* (1980), and *Treasury of Literature for Children* (1984). It was even included in an Edwardian collection of naval ballads as a typical example from Dartmoor.[43]

Alec Guinness referenced Cobley in his autobiography, as did Agatha Christie and Peter Cushing. Likewise, Nancy Mitford, Richard Burton, Bernard Shaw, Philip Larkin, P. G. Wodehouse and Rupert Brooke referred to him in letters and Spike Milligan cited Tom Cobley in an interview with Groucho Marx.[44] Dylan Thomas referred to the mare's riders in a letter in which he wrote 'I wouldn't share a piston with Stephen [Spender] or Wystan [Auden] but I'd roll in a sewer with Jan and Bill Brewer'.[45] It also featured in James Joyce's *Finnegan's Wake* as well as in a story by Rudyard Kipling (his characters sang 'Bill Brewer, Sam Sewer') and in a play by John Osborne; the latter changed the lyrics to 'Harold Pinter, Harold Pinter, lend me your grey mare'.[46]

It has also had incarnations on stage and in films. In 1905 M. P. Wilcocks published *Widdicombe*, a novel set in Devon but not in Widecombe-in-the-Moor. It may be that she used Baring-Gould's archaic spelling because it was familiar to potential book buyers but the plot and settings have no correlation with the ballad.[47] Eight years later, in 1913, Eden Phillpotts, another established Devon writer, published *Widecombe Fair*, a novel which was based on the song. This 'modest comedy of Dartmoor' was, according to one reviewer, 'a close study of the people of an entrancing part of the country'. Cobley was one of the characters as was Harry Hawke.[48] A silent film based on the play was released in 1929 and featured Moore Marriott as Cobley; alongside him appeared his fellow excursionists.[49]

Two years later 1,300 pensioners gathered at the 'Oldest Inhabitants New Year

MOORE MARRIOT

UNCLE TOM COBLEIGH AND ALL.

Moore Marriott as Cobley, 1928.

Festivities' at Southend. A journalist reported that the audience greatly enjoyed the entertainment except for one disgruntled octogenarian who was finally challenged to perform himself. George Smith, said to be 84, peevish and petulant, responded with his version of 'Widdicombe Fair'. He brought the house down and was required to sing the song twice more at which point Smith 'collapsed' and was taken off stage. It transpired that his real identity was Marriott, then aged 45, who had arranged the ruse with the theatre manager. Marriott said: 'I did it to please the old folks, and I have never enjoyed an act with greater gusto. They loved it and so did I. The most surprising thing of the business is that no one knew me.' The theatre manager said 'It was the cleverest and jolliest *put over* I have ever seen'.[50]

The literary popularity of 'Widdicombe Fair' has extended to translations in Arabic and at least three continental languages: it was translated into Spanish in 1931, Italian in the early 1940s and French in 1948.[51] In 1900 the ballad was written in prose. The writer used considerable imagination in describing the company of riders.

Reasons for popularity and endurance

The tune of 'Widdicombe Fair' was in itself popular. Baring-Gould used the music he had from William Collier in preference to that he heard sung by Harry Westaway. In 1930 Sir Charles Pinkham, of Membland near Newton Ferrers, recalled having met Westaway many years earlier at a public house in Belstone:

> Somebody told me to call upon old Farmer Westaway for a song. *Come on Farmer Westaway*, I said, *let us have a good old Devon song. Why, damn sir,* he replied *I should like to but I be mortal dry.* I put that right and old Westaway said. *I'll sing 'ee* Uncle Tom Cobleigh and All, *like my grandfather and his grandfather sang it years ago before old Baring-Gould got messing it about and setting it to music.*[52]

Other variants had their own tunes: of 'Stow Fair' it was said in 1936 that it had 'a better tune but the words not so good' while 'Midsummer Fair' was noted at the same time as having 'more character and a better rhythm'.[53] (Version 16a) The music of 'Widdicombe Fair' was continually adapted, as in 1916 when Julius Harrison, an English composer known for opera, wrote it as 'a humoresque quartet for strings' and in 1921 when it became a piano duet.[54]

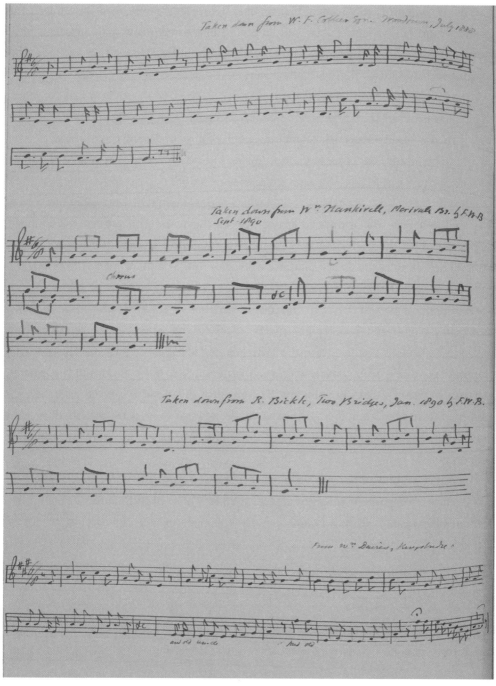

The music for three versions as sent to Baring-Gould, 1888.

The viability of seven men riding one horse was questioned not long after 'Widdicombe Fair' was published[55] and a generation later a group of Moroccans heard the song but remained puzzled about the riders. About this time a London journalist imagined a future historian would discover:

> Whence came the now general belief that Old Uncle Tom Cobley, with Bill
> Brewer, Jan Struther [sic], Peter Gurney, Peter Fleming [sic] and three or four
> others all rode on the back of the grey mare instead of driving her in the cart.

Despite being unsure of the details, the reporter was right: the lyrics do not specify that the men rode the unnamed mare.[56] Some illustrators have been unsuccessful in placing all of the men on her while others, including Stanley Baker and Pamela Colman Smith, illustrated the ballad with a wagon. At least one version of the song, as will be seen, specified that the men travelled in a cart. (Version 17)

The Feniton version of 1867 in unusual in that it describes the mare as being feeble and old. (Version 9) It has been suggested that the grey mare harks back to the tradition of a ghost horse which brings riders on a path to their deaths. Comparisons have been drawn with Welsh Mari Lywd, hobbyhorses and the many Dartmoor tales of other ghost horses. The ghost of the horse was often referred to as 'gashly', meaning ghastly.[57] The noise it made was 'skirling', that is a shrill wailing tone. Irrespective of its meaning, the ghostly appearance of the mare increased the ballad's appeal.

Finally, the song imparts a sense of comaraderie and this is increased when the names of the company of riders are substituted for those of individuals known to the audience.

The chorus and its adaptions

> *With Bill Brewer, Jan Stewer, Peter Gurney, Peter Davy, Dan'l Whiddon, Harry Hawk*
> *Old Uncle Tom Cobbleigh and all*
> *Old Uncle Tom Cobbleigh and all.*

The chorus, or as it was once more commonly termed its 'burden', enhanced the interest in 'Widdicombe Fair'. This concluding verse was noted in 1901 by one writer as holding 'the palm for the longiest, funniest and most quaintly-apropos double burden in existence'. Furthermore, it was postulated that it 'is so indispensible a part of the narrative that it almost forgoes its normal role of a mere accessory'.[58] A later writer also recognised this in 1921:

> 'No better illustration could be given of the way in which the singers of folk
> songs have in all ages altered the words thereof to get the turn of the market,
> so to speak, and of their very human motives for so doing. Such changes made
> for a renewal of popularity; they helped to convince the hearer that he was
> listening to a true tale. After all, the songs were the property of the people
> who sang them and they had a right to make such alterations from time to
> time as seemed proper and profitable. An old song which nobody cared to
> hear would have been a mere curio.'[59]

Substitutions resonated with audiences in such places as Beer, Washford Pyne, Chillaton, Whimple and Tawstock where the singer 'introduced the names of local characters'.[60] A typical reaction was one in the East Devon village of Plymtree in 1932:

> The hit of the evening was Mr Rhill's opening song, Honiton Fair,
> substituting that of the usual Widdicombe Fair, and instead of the usual Bill
> Brewer, Jan Stewer, etc. he used the names of the Dons of the village which
> amused everyone while his final line of *Old Uncle Will Prouse and all* fairly
> brought the house down.[61]

At Torquay in 1895 the names of local football players were sung. Occasionally substitutions were recorded such as in 1895 at the Masonic lodge at Exmouth the first verse was:

> Sam Bennetts, Sam Bennetts, lend me your grey mare
>> All along, down along, out along lee
> For I want to go to Widdicombe Fair
>> With Bert B., Sam F., Dick G., Harry C., Tom H., Will. P., Uncle Jack P. and all
>> Uncle Jack D. and all.[62]

In 1905 Devonians who lived in Eastbourne also adapted the song at a public dinner:

All along, down along, out along, lay

    For I want to go to Widdycombe Fair

With Doctor Adams, Doctor Willoughby, Muster Glanfield, Muster Lerwill,

        Muster Fryer, Old Uncle Tom Cobleigh and all

    Old Uncle Tom Cobleigh and all.[63]

Similar groups are known to have performed in a like manner in Cambridge, Birmingham, Worcester, Liverpool, Bath, London and Leicester as well as Sydney, Winnipeg, Montreal and Calcutta.[64]

In 1928 in Bristol there was an equally unusual substitution at a meeting of the employees of J. S. Fry & Company, the chocolate manufacturers:

> An interesting little diversion from the ordinary choruses of one of the songs
> "Widdicombe Fair" was made. Instead of roaring those well-known names,
> Bill Brewer, Jan Stewer, Peter Gurney, Peter Davy, etc., the company in the
> community singing sang the names of employees of the firm who had 50
> years service to their credit, and this proved immensely popular with the
> audience.[65]

These choruses amused audiences across England. In 1889 a mothers' meeting in a London church heard 'an odd refrain' in which the singer added to the audience's amusement 'the name of each mother'.[66] Great Yarmouth was another far-flung location where local names delighted audiences[67] and by 1935 the song was adapted for football supporters at Sunderland:

> John Cochrane, John Cochrane, things are looking up.
>   All along, down along, all along lee
> We'll see the team winning the League and the Cup
>   With Jimmy Connor, Horatio Carter, Bobby Gurney, Bert Davis,
>   Patsy Gallacher,
>   And Uncle Joe Prior and all![68]

Prior was then Chairman of Sunderland AFC and the remaining individuals were players. In 1920 the chorus reflected members of England's cricket team who were sailing to Australia for the Ashes.[69]

John Collings Squire, a writer and Plymothian by birth, wrote an unusual imitator in 1917. His poem entitled 'No. 7 Numerous Celts' concludes 'With Pat Doogan, Father Murphy, Brown maidens, King Cuchullain, the Kine, the Sheep, some old women, some old men and Uncle White Sea-gull and all.'[70]

The ballad was adapted with a difference in 1907 for a Christmas play in Dorchester-on-Thames. It included the lines:

> From the vicar through all kind-hearted men, as Santa Claus, Father
> Christmas, Anderson, Dan Leno, Charles Dickens, Peter Tavy, Corelli, Sam
> Snapdragon, Boy Gravy, Mike Mistletoe, with Mince Pie, Bob Snowball,
> Russell Sage, Uncle Tom Cobleigh and All.[71]

Cobley's idiom

'And Uncle Tom Cobley & All'

The final verse came to define an exasperating list of people. On the face of it, Karl Marx appears to have been the earliest writer to use this expression. An edition of his letters shows that in 1859 he wrote from London to Friedrich Engels:

> During my absence debts have been contracted amounting to over six
> pounds, since the agents, printer, old Uncle Tom Cobley and all suspected that
> my return would put an end to the fun.

However, this translation by his English editors is misleading. Marx had written in German *'Gott und der Teufel ahnten'* by which he meant 'God and the Devil'. The editors substituted this in 1983 for what they thought was an English equivalent.'[72]

However, H. G. Wells was one who did use this device ('the Jews and the King and Queen and the Pope and Mr Stalin and the Mikado, Mr Chamberlain, Adolf Hitler, Uncle Tom Cobleigh and all'). So too have Angus Wilson, Len Deighton, Sean O'Casey, George Macdonald Fraser, Catherine Cookson, John Le Carre, Dorothy L. Sayers and Noel Coward.[73]

The list 'uncontrolled dosing of children, old people, animals, Uncle Tom Cobley and all' was written by Germaine Greer, 'Kirk Douglas, Hermione Gingold, Nureyev and old Uncle Tom Cobleigh' was used in 1973 to describe stars in a television

Tom Pearce is asked to borrow his mare, by Pamela Colman Smith, 1898.

programme, and a similar list ('Elizabeth Taylor, Cher, Catherine Deneuve, Victoria Principal, Linda Evans, Mikhail Baryshnikov, Omar Sharif, Sophia Loren and Uncle Tom Cobley and All') was penned by Joan Collins to note contemporaries who had launched their own lines of perfume.[74]

Many other instances of the adapted list of names can be cited. In 1931, for instance when Albert Einstein was identified as demonic: 'he is Sheltan, Lucifer, Belial, Arimanius, Samael, Beelzebub, Apollyon and I am by no means sure that he isn't Old Uncle Tom Cobleigh and All'. It was likewise deployed at Eastbourne to refer to bathing machine operators ('J. A. Hounsom, T. Hounsom, Sam Erridge, Peter

Gowland and Uncle Tom Cobleigh and All') and at a meeting of the Showmen's Guild in Westminster which had 'Mr Bertram Mills (described as *the circus man*), Mr W. E. Butlin (the biggest provider of amusements at the seaside), Mr Patrick Collins (the *king of travelling showmen*), Mr W. Wilson (of *World's Fair* fame), Uncle Tom Cobleigh and All'.[75] Meanwhile, in 1935 Kent Carnival was said to have included 'John Bull, Sunny Jim, the Queen of Hearts, gay Robin Hood, Harlequin and Columbine, Old Uncle Tom Cobley and All'.[76]

Other uses have linked Cobley with equally unusual companions. 'Cliff Richard, ABBA, Henry Kissinger, Judy Garland, Mel Brooks, Sammy Davis Junior, Old Uncle Tom Cobley and All' was used in the *Rough Guide to Scandinavia* to explain the guests

The mare pulls a cart to Widecombe-on-the-Moor, by Pamela Colman Smith, 1898.

Widecombe Fair, by Pamela Colman Smith, 1898.

in one particular Swedish hotel while he was referenced alongside Hitler and Mussolini in *The Eagle Has Landed*. He was combined with Julius Caesar, Napoleon Bonaparte, Lenin and Mussolini in a Parliamentary debate and the Home Secretary and a Soviet spy used the line 'the Attorney General, the Lord Chief Justice, Uncle Tom Cobley and All'.[77] In 1964 the Deputy Labour Leader claimed that the Liberals would sacrifice 'EFTA, the Commonwealth agriculture and old Uncle Tom Cobley and all' in order to gain access to the Common Market.[78]

Similar verses were used to refer to The Book Society, the 'celebrity' society that recommended books from 1929:

> Oh, it's lovely to think as you lie in your bed
> With a couple of pillows to prop up your head
> That the book you are reading has also been read by Hugh Walpole, Clemence
> Dane, Sylvia Lind, George Gordon, (Professor Gordon from Oxford)
>   And Johnny B. Priestley and all
>   And Johnny B. Priestley and all.[79]

Tom Pearce looks for his mare, by Pamela Colman Smith, 1898.

The mare is found dead, by Pamela Colman Smith, 1898.

Another unusual example relates to a change in interior design in 1934 when it became fashionable to place pictures on walls.

> I see that our pictures are back on the wall
>> A-hiding the old distemper
> And now, once again, we can gaze upon all
>> Our relations Aunt Ethel, Cousin Cissy, Little Georgie,
>>> Old Uncle Tom Cobleigh and all
>>> Old Uncle Tom Cobleigh and all.[80]

Perhaps its most unusual incarnation has been in academic publications to note a string of authors instead of the standard phrase *et al.* For example, Cobley was cited in the 1973 issue of the *Journal of the American Chemical Society*; in this U. T. Cobley is one of eight authors credited with writing 'Applications of photoelectron spectroscopy 41'.[81] Likewise he might be confused with being a contributor to 'The bimolecular self-reactions of secondary peroxy radicals'.[82]

This device has also extended beyond personal names; in 1932 a gardener commented that he left his garden to 'all the dark subversive elements in the soil, the chickweed, wireworms, leather-jackets, red ants, gooseberry mildew and Uncle Tom Cobley and all'. Likewise, in 1926 the noises found on country roads were 'honk-honk (the motor bike, and another and some more), par-par, gor-gor (a Ford with its Sunday smile on), haw-haw, honk-gor, honk, honk, haw (Morris Cowley, young Morgan, bright Sunbeam, smart Daimler, Old Uncle Tom Cobley and All)'.[83]

During the Great War the phrase was used in France. A visitor wrote:

At Marseilles it was bright morning, and I was lucky enough to get a pannier, at a trifling cost of seven francs. These panniers are no meal for a hungry man. They contain a bone of chicken, a scrap of ham, a corner of Gruyere, a stick of bread (that surely was made by the firm that put the sand in sandwich), a half bottle of sour white wine, a bottle of the eternal Vichy, Old Uncle Tom Cobleigh and all.[84]

The Second World War threw up more peculiar instances. In 1937 a Yeovil commentator on air raid precautions thought it unlikely the Germans would unleash gas attacks on rural English villages; he felt that the First World War anthem *Gott strafe England* (May God punish England) would not be '*Gott strafe* Bill Brewer, Jan Stewer… old Uncle Tom Cobley and all'. Two years later a Brummie commentator noted that heavy fog hid Birmingham from 'Herr Hitler, Hermann Goering, Rudolf Hess, *Marse* Goebbels, Mr Brauchitsch, Admiral Raeder and Uncle Tom Cobley and all'.[85]

In 1941 an observer of the fighting in the Balkans recorded they had a column of 'bren [machine guns], medium and light tanks, mobile artillery, armoured cars and motor cycles, signallers, sappers and Uncle Tom Cobleigh and all' while a year later another war correspondent wrote that on the Pacific Front 'airmen, ground staffs, machines, para-troops and Uncle Tom Cobley and all are getting ready or are already moving, east.'[86] That same year I. B. Batz, formerly known as E. B. Crackers of Lewes, wrote to a Sussex newspaper about German bombing on Sundays; he commented that he had sent similar letters to 'the Prime Minister, General Wavell, President Roosevelt, Mr Eden, General Timoschenko, Comrade Stalin, Mr Schickelgruber and Old Uncle Tom Cobley and All'.[87]

Cobley made many other appearances such as when the Minister of Agriculture stated in the House of Commons that common land would be put to agricultural use by 'un-interned aliens, interned aliens, schoolboys, prisoners, members of the Pioneer Corps and Uncle Tom Cobley and All'. In 1940 a newspaper columnist described Hollywood's young stars as being 'Ann Rutherford, Mickey Rooney, Judy Garland, Robert Stack, Linda Darnell and Uncle Tom Cobley and All' while a similar list comprised 'Robert Taylor, Wallace Beery, Errol Flynn, Jimmy Cagney and Uncle Tom Cobleigh and All'. In 1945 Barnstaple's new Member of Parliament thanked 'Jack Isaac, Harry Pincombe, Tom Anstey and a thousand and one others – in fact in the West Country vernacular, Uncle Tom Cobley and all'.[88]

Post war Britain continued the practice: an astrological forecast for September 1945 held that Jupiter would be in opposition to 'the Licensing Laws, Utility Suits, the Points System, the Education Act, Pay-As-You-Earn, the Einstein theory and Old Uncle Tom Cobley and All'. A subsequent reference to politics at Westminster included the phrase 'Herbert Morrison, Nye Bevan, the Secretary of the Football Association, Winston Churchill or Uncle Tom Cobleigh'.[89] The phrase continues in modern usage such as when used in a recent episode of Newsnight, a news story in the *Irish Times* and in many novels.[90]

Tom Cobley

The identity of the original Tom Cobley has been questioned since the publication of 'Widdicombe Fair'. In 1911 one writer commented 'There is no Devonshire celebrity whose name is wider known and yet of whose personality so little is known as Old Uncle Tom Cobley or Cobleigh'.[91] Even so, it has not impeded his taking many guises during those 130 years. The spelling of his name has also differed (Cobble, Cobbley, Cobleigh and Cobbleigh amongst others) with Cobley being the most commonly used now.

Origins

Baring-Gould was confident of Cobley's identity. He thought:

> The original Uncle Tom Cobley lived in a house near Yeoford Junction in the
> parish of Spreyton. His will was signed on January 20th 1787 and was proved
> on March 14th 1794. He was a genial old bachelor. Mr Samuel Peach [sic], his
> eldest relative living, tells me *my great uncle, who succeeded him, with whom*
> *he lived for years, died in 1843 over 80 years of age. He married but left no*
> *children.*[92]

This Tom Cobley has also been called a 'rascal'; a scrapbook allegedly once kept in
Coleford had a note 'He signed a document to the effect that he would be responsible
for the upkeep of redheaded children only. He was himself famous apparently for a
carroty head'.[93]

Newspaper reports noted him as 'the glory of Colebrooke' who kept a pack of
harriers at Butsford and was referred to by journalists as Uncle Tom Cobley between
1828 and 1842. He died in 1844 and was buried in Spreyton's churchyard.[94]

Even earlier was the Uncle Tom Cobley associated with the Devon artist Benjamin
R. Haydon; he served in the Russian army and his estate at Odessa was called Cobleska.
He died in 1834.[95]

Subsequent research has determined there were up to six men by the name of Tom
Cobley in the Spreyton area from 1698 to 1844.[96] However, Crediton has also laid claim
to him. In 1682 Thomas Cobley, the son of another Thomas Cobley, was baptised in
the parish church. Thomasine, the daughter of John Cobley, was also baptised there
in 1680 but was buried at Spreyton in 1698. Crediton's parish register also includes
individuals with the surnames Davey, Hawkes, Pearse and Stewer and this led to one
writer to conclude 'Crediton was the original home not only of old Uncle Tom but
also of the band of friends who accompanied him on his famous expedition'.[97] It may
be that Cobley was not a Devonian: in the early 1800s there were nearly three dozen
men named Tom Cobley resident in counties across England. Not only were there half
a dozen in Colebrooke, Brixham and Topsham but there were others in Somerset,
London, Huntingdonshire, Leicestershire, Northamptonshire, Rutlandshire and
Warwickshire. Berkshire may have previously considered him one of its own: in 1902
and 1905 'A Reminiscence of Uncle Tom Cobley' was given in the local dialect.[98]

It is likely that the song was the reason for an Exonian with the name Thomas Cobley having been renamed by 1870. A journalist noted this auctioneer's assistant 'was a well known and popular character and was generally spoken of by the familiar appellation of *Uncle* Tom Cobley'. It was also because of the ballad that in the early 1900s the landlord of The Warren Inn, on Dartmoor, was known as Uncle Tom Cobley.[99] 'Uncle Tom' was the name given to E. T. Langdon who retired as a London constable in 1912. He was given that name not only because he was, in his own words, a 'Devonshire Dumpling' but also because he continually sang the ballad. Not long after this 'Uncle Cobley' was the nickname of Clarence Stanley Goode, the director of the BBC station at Plymouth.[100]

Impersonators

For nearly a century Cobley has attended Widecombe Fair dressed in antiquated rustic clothing. Edward Dunn was the first impersonator and from 1928 to 1937 he became a highly visible and popular attraction at the fair. He was followed by Robert Dunn (1938), Albert Dunn (1945–8), William Miners, (1949), Tom Hext (1950), Jack Brown (1951–7), Simon Northmore (1958-81), Gordon Daw (1982-5), Peter Hicks (1986–96) and Tony Deeble (1997–2000, 2002–).

Beatrice Chase, a novelist resident in the village in the early 1900s, laid claim to the idea. In 1948 she wrote:

> 'I am really proud to say it was I, years ago, who started the Old Uncle Tom
> Cobley procession, by presenting a genuine smock frock from Norfolk to
> Mr Dunn. This gave him the idea of impersonating that famous gentleman
> and now his son, Mr Albert Dunn, carries on the tradition and does it
> splendidly.'[101]

Two authors independently assumed Cobley's identity. Walter Raymond, who lived in Yeovil in Somerset, published as Tom Cobbleigh from 1892 until his death in 1931. His novels included *Gentleman Upcott's Daughter*. From 1907 a Devon vicar, Edward Robert Gotto, used a variant spelling (Tom Cobleigh) as his pseudonym for such books as *Zum Vunny Demshur Tellins* and *Down in Devon: umorous tales*.[102]

During the Second World War an anonymous Hull donor to the war effort used Cobley as his moniker. The *Hull Daily Mail* routinely reported his donations and

Edward Dunn as Cobley with 'Uncle Tom Cobley's Chair', *c*1928–37.

referred to this gentleman as 'our dear old friend'. He began in February 1940 by giving six mouth organs to 'the lads in France' and later donated books, an electronic iron and darts before the *nom de plume* was taken over by a group of individuals who sent gifts of a billiard table, deck chairs and sets of chessmen. These 'anonymous pals of all serving men' subsequently provided musical instruments to the men who had lost them at Dunkirk and continued to give through to the end of the war. They may have been members of the Devon & Cornwall Society, all of whom originated from the two counties. It had been formed in 1926. In 1939 a Hull soldier in France requested the sheet music for 'Widdicombe Fair'. Newspaper readers were told 'the boys in France want to sing'.[103]

Most recently, in the 1950s Dennis Gleeson wrote two plays concerned with contemporary working-class life for the Unity Theatre in London under the name Tom Cobley.[104]

Jan Stewer

A. J. Coles impersonated Stewer during the first half of the twentieth century. Coles was a schoolteacher who had been born at Woolwich in 1876 but moved to Devon to work in Puddington. He began writing a column, *The Talk at Uncle Tom Cobleigh's Club*, on 2 March 1900 in the *Exeter & Plymouth Gazette*. Coles wrote as Stewer without a break for fifty years and became a Devon celebrity. By the time of his death, in 1965, he had written more than 2,500 stories in dialect. Some were republished as books. Coles also wrote 'Barnet's Folly Day', which was at the Haymarket Theatre in London in 1935 before it toured, with Coles as one of the actors, across the country. He also performed in character widely throughout Devon. Coles was not the first to promote Devon dialect, he was preceded by 'Peter Pindar' (John Wolcot), 'Nathan Hogg' (Elias Tozer) and 'Tickler (Henry Baird) but he became the most celebrated writer of Devon dialect.[105]

The other characters have had a lower public profile although Stewer, Peter Gurney and Harry Hawke were brought to life in 1926 for a mock trial in Birmingham organised by the Midland Devonian Society and the Midland Cornish Association. They prosecuted three Cornishmen over their use of the term 'The Riviera'.[106]

Tourism

Devon's guidebooks invariably mention Tom Cobley when noting Widecombe-in-the-Moor. In 1927 one visitor noted:

> I never realised the power of song till I came to Widecombe! Four charabancs
> were drawn up opposite the village green. Old Uncle Tom Cobleigh stood
> leaning on an ash stick, his back bent, watching from the green the swift
> descent of the trippers with their cameras. Young men and young women
> roamed vaguely arm in arm through the lanes, languishingly or gaily
> according to temperament. Elderly women swarmed over the church; men in
> holiday humour sampled the village inn. A hen crossed the road delicately, as
> if trying to avoid the cameras.[107]

A Cobley industry has taken the form of souvenir postcards, lapel badges, jigsaw puzzles, horse brasses, doorknockers, ashtrays, thimbles, caddy spoons, bowls, teapots, butter dishes, egg cups, pie funnels, trinket boxes, serving trays, plates, tea cups, figures, mugs, tankards and jugs. Cobley has even had his own brands of gin (Uncle Tom Cobley's Sloe Gin) and whisky (Uncle Tom Cobley's Scotch Whisky). Advertisers have used his name to endorse products such as matches, cigarettes, motor oil and ale.[108]

Despite the uncertainties of Cobley's identity, relics have emerged including his bible and a walking stick which was shown to visitors in the early 1930s. His chair has moved around Widecombe, including in the church, until it was placed in a gift shop.[109] In 1935 a group of scouts visited the village and reported:

> One shop declare they have the original Uncle Tom Cobleigh's favourite chair,
> a rival shop says that last year the chair was just an antique and then someone
> had a brainwave and called it Uncle Tom Cobleigh's chair.[110]

Ten years later it was discovered:

> In the village there is an old manor house set aside as a Tom Cobley museum.
> It is well worth looking at. Here there are hundreds of little trinkets and
> postcards for sale and on view an old chair which was one of Tom's most

THE TATLER AND BY'TANDER, APRIL 9. 1947

Mare and Corporation

Tom Pearce, Tom Pearce, will you tell us what course
    (All along, out along, down along lea)
You took to develop the thews of a horse,
    Like Carnera, Goliath, Eugene Sandow, Gog and Magog,
    Paul Bunyan, Asar Thor,
    And Popeye the Sailor and all, and Popeye the Sailor and all.

My mare, you remember, so lately deceased,
    (By the terms of her will I'm the sole legatee)
Was in several respects a remarkable beast,
    Like Bucephalus, Prince Regent, Hrimfaxi, Copenhagen,
    Black Beauty, Brown Bess,
    (Eohippus was rather too small, Eohippus was rather too small.)

Although, being horse, she could not herself sing,
    A prop of the opera nightly was she,
For she carried the diva through most of The Ring,
    And Tannhäuser, Don Juan, Leonora, Traviata, Trovatore, Pagliacci,
    And old Uncle Siegfried and all, and old Uncle Siegfried and all.

She died ; and to carry the vast prima-donna
    (Seventeen stone) now devolved upon me.
" Bring Guinness ! " I cried, " or Tom Pearce is a gonner !
Not zibbib, nor arrak, nor toddy, nor metheglin, nor date-beer, nor tedj
Bring Guinness or nothing at all ! Bring Guinness or nothing at all."

The dame was amazed by her spirited mount,
    And ever since then I'm a strong devotee
Of Guinness, whose virtues are quite without count,
    And for goodness, and richness, body-building,
    Frame-filling, muscle-making, good health,
    A Guinness is good for us all, a Guinness is good for us all.

Advertising by Guinness using the story of Tom Pearce and a diva at the opera, 1947.

valuable possessions. The chair is said to be 400 years old and it is beautifully carved with dragon's heads for arms.[111]

This chair is similar in style to one in Plympton St Mary's parish church. There are other 'Cobley' chairs at Spreyton and Crediton.[112]

A public house in Spreyton was renamed The Tom Cobley Tavern in about 1970 but it has no connection with a national chain of 'Tom Cobleigh' pubs which began operation two decades later.[113]

The chair attributed to Tom Cobley.

TWO

The ballad's history

'Widdicombe Fair' triumphed when it became recognised as Devon's anthem but its success has obscured a long and fascinating history in which many variants have been sung not only in Devon but much further afield.

The report of a performance in the Feniton Inn of 'Uncle Tam Cobley and All', a previously unnoticed version which is twenty-one years earlier than that published by Baring-Gould, sheds light into ballad singing in Victorian Devon in general but also into this particular song. In 1867 a Devon journalist, who had an interest in music, attended a 'Club Day' in East Devon. George Pulman watched a procession of 'clubbists' from the Feniton Friendly Society enter the Anglican Church of St Andrew. He understood the purpose of the day, in citing Psalm 133, was 'to show *How good and pleasant a thing it is for brethren to dwell together in unity*'.[114] Pulman noted that the men walked two abreast:

> with music and a banner, each man bearing on his holiday bosom a gay
> rosette and carrying a stave, the practical use of which I fail to discover. The
> old men come first (one venerable rustic being, I am told, ninety years of age)
> and the young ones follow after.

Pulman participated in the church service which included Edward Marks, the parish clerk who was also the postmaster.[115] Marks reportedly 'fired' off Amens 'like the crack of a rifle'. Pulman then noted that after the service the clubbists went to:

38

their substantial dinner which is laid for them by Host Darke in his capacious
skittle alley. Here the band (from Colyton) and about eighty persons assemble
with appetites that require no sauce to tickle them. I sit by the side of the old
gentleman of ninety who has a chubby-faced grandson on his knee.

Once the meal finished Mr Toogood,[116] 'a respected yeoman', gave the toasts,
complimented the Society and called upon:

> several *zinging faces* to justify their harmonious appearance. Venerable Marks
> hath very nearly reached the appointed age of man, but he sings in the shrill
> treble of his youth. The songs are rural in pattern, indifferent to rhyme but
> very powerful in the sentiment of affection. One has reference to *Charming
> Molly* who appeals to *Constant Johnny* to free her from a single life, which she
> appears to regard as a very irksome and unnatural mode of existence. The
> band plays at intervals and women, some with babies, enter the capacious
> building to participate with their husbands and sweethearts in the pleasures
> of the afternoon.

Most interestingly of his observances, Pulman recorded one song in detail. He
wrote that 'one old gentleman, whose pipes he tells me are nearly worn out, gratifies
me intensely by humming the following ditty.' This version of 'Widdicombe Fair' has
six verses in which the names of the company are different and the men travelled
to Hoodycock Fair via Hoodycock Hill.(Version 9) It is, as will be discussed in the
following pages, part of the rich history of the ballad.

The singers

In 1888 Baring-Gould obtained the ballad's lyrics from William Collier of Horrabridge.
They had recently been dinner companions in Tavistock and the conversation turned
to the gradual loss of old local songs. Their host suggested that the cleric was best
placed to record Devon's songs 'It is a sad thing that our folk music should perish.
I wish you would set to work and collect it – gather up the fragments that remain
before all is lost!' Baring-Gould took up the challenge with great enthusiasm and later
regarded it to have been the principal achievement of his life.[117]

By this date folk songs had been collected elsewhere in England but only irregularly in Devon. Baring-Gould's collection began with Collier's contribution, which is fitting given its subsequent fame. He most likely sent the lyrics on 15 September. Baring-Gould then appealed beyond his fellow diners; he wrote to the editor of *The Western Antiquary* asking the public to contribute information. The result was, he wrote, a 'deluge' of variants of 'Widdicombe Fair'; some twenty versions were sent.[118]

Baring-Gould's notebooks show that he and his colleagues subsequently collected songs from a great number of individuals. Variants of 'Widdicombe Fair' came from William Davies of Kingsbridge, William Nankivell of Merrivale, Richard Bickle of Two Bridges, F. J. Adams at Kingsbridge and Henry Westaway of Belstone. Others came via newspapers and from his social equals but Baring-Gould realised the importance of talking to the 'singing men' who performed the ballads in public houses and at local fairs.

In addition to this, Devon in 1889, like the rest of England, had a long tradition of street singing. For instance, in 1884 one local newspaper reported that 'the street songs of the moment, the sensation which everybody enjoys, are over the crew that ate the boy at sea.' Two seamen from the *Mignonette* were then being prosecuted at Rougemont Castle for cannibalism. Songs were also regularly composed in rural parishes in order to ridicule or castigate those who were thought to have offended public morals. This happened at Sandy Gate in Exeter in 1857 when a mob of forty neighbours targeted one woman. They banged tin kettles, burned an effigy, shouted 'come out you old bitch, we'll burn your body, bones and all' and then serenaded her with a balled which had a chorus 'catch me if you can'. The tradition of ridiculing in song goes back in Devon to at least the early 1500s.[119]

Likewise, in 1832 two Devon printers appeared in court over a libellous ballad entitled 'The wanton tradesman of Devonport' which was sung to the tune of 'Heigh Ho Billy'. It had swept through Devonport.

> Come all ye *bill buyers* and listen to me
> I'll sing you a song that shall fill you with glee
> Concerning a hero, a Jew-looking chap
> Who a......'s wife kiss'd and was thrash'd with the strap
> > Heigh ho! Billy, Billy, *Ill-fated* Billy
> > Beware of the husband, when you kiss the wife.

To his neighbouring tradesmen he is a disgrace
And 'tis strange he can look any one in the face
All who know him dislike him, his tricks they like worse
And his character, therefore, is not worth a curse
    Heigh ho! Billy, Billy, Ill-fated Billy
    Beware of the husband, when you kiss the wife.

You surely must know who I mean to describe
He's one of the blarneying hypocrite tribe
Now if to learn more you have any desires
He's one of the *Sellers* and one of the *Buyers*
    Heigh ho! Billy, Billy, Ill-fated Billy
    Beware of the husband, when you kiss the wife.

Moral

Now all you gay fellows who value your lives
Pray never go meddling with other men's wives
For the husband when injured will never give in
'Till he's broken each ill-fated bone in your skin
    Heigh ho! Billy, Billy, Ill-fated Billy
    Beware of the husband, when you kiss the wife.

There was subsequent uncertainty other whether a black eye had been caused by a printer falling against a shop counter or if it was due to the attentions of the wronged party.[120]

A few years previously another ballad was composed in Cullompton. William Melhuish, a miller and baker, objected to the allegation that he was 'guilty of a filthy and disgusting practice in making his bread'. It had been implied that he mixed clay with his dough but this was only one of the allegations in the ballad:

Who, to make his bread more nice
On the dough board cracks his children's lice
And mix them with his cakes for spice?

A covered cart brought through the streets accompanied the singing of the ballad. On it was a loaf with a sign 'warranted free from lice and rotten teeth'; Melhuish's wife had reportedly been seen checking her children's heads in the bakery shop.[121]

Ballads were sung not only in the streets but also in public concerts by professional singers. In 1842 Adelaide Kemble, a national performer, sang ballads at the Royal Clarence in Exeter. A journalist reported her 'wonderful impassioned feeling struck everyone with astonishment – the compass of her voice being only equalled by the depth of her feeling. She sang like one inspired.' Kemble's respectability was uncompromised by an unusual personal habit. It was reported that 'Miss A. Kemble is a cigar smoker. A professional gentleman of this city, on being introduced to her, was honoured with the offer of a cigar from her case.'[122] Her ballads were ones appropriate to concert halls and drawing rooms.

In contrast, in 1862 'street songs' were performed at the Mechanics' Institute in Torquay by Fourness Rolfe, who had heard them 'chanted in the streets' by what were described as 'itinerant ballad singers'. Most interestingly, Rolfe had reproduced their likenesses on canvas.[123]

There was an aversion to performing these and other traditional songs in middle class company. Perhaps not surprisingly, it was from Sidmouth that such sentiments were expressed in 1868 about a concert, which had:

> So attractive a programme without having recourse, for popularity's sake, to
> any of those comic street songs which, however amusing they may be, and
> however secure of commanding applause, always require, if admitted at all
> on these occasions, no ordinary amount of tact and delicacy of delivery, to
> prevent their proving deleterious, and seem to me always to carry us rather
> more near than is desirable to the confines of the public house.[124]

In 1838 Exeter's Lammas Fair, which was held along the river, was described as a country fair and had a number of features common with other fairs such as pugilists and gambling tables. Particularly popular were the booths where men and women not only drank and smoked but enjoyed 'rude songs'. Such singing could be prosecuted when it took place in the open streets. This happened in 1835 to Mrs Worth, an Exeter shell fish vendor, and to Bridget Grainger, an Irish pedlar, of whom it was later said in Barnstaple 'her language was most indecent, worse than he had ever heard in his life from any man, and she continued sometimes bawling, sometimes singing, the most obscene songs'.[125] Likewise, in 1870 two men, noted as street singers, were charged with singing obscene ballads in the public streets of Torquay. In another instance, Exeter's 'Uncle Ned' was prosecuted in 1856 for selling ballads 'of the grossest character'. These, he claimed, had originated in Plymouth and were typical of the more vulgar broadsides, which were commonly sold.[126]

Baring-Gould sought out similar men and women in the South West. He later recollected that:

> At first I went to the farmers and yeomen but soon ascertained that no
> material of any value for my purpose was to be obtained from them… It was
> necessary to drop to a lower level if we were to tap the spring of traditional
> folk music. I speedily discovered that what I wanted was to be obtained
> mainly from such men as could neither read nor write.[127]

The cleric concluded that every village inn had a singer who was rewarded for his amusing songs with free drinks. When documented in newspapers such ballad singers were invariably connected with being intoxicated. This included William Harris in Devonport in 1863 and William Jones in Tavistock in 1882.[128] Baring-Gould interviewed similar singers. Altogether he, and a number of collaborators, interviewed 189 singers of whom 29 were women. The best-known woman was Sally Satterley whose father was an 'old cripple singing man'. A Victorian writer summarised this Dartmoor woman:

> She was during the greater part of her life in work usually performed by men.
> She was for some time employed in the mine at Eylesbarrow, drove pack
> horses, could cut peat, was able to mow with a scythe and… could nail a
> shoe to a horse's hoof as well as a blacksmith. She was probably the last of her
> kind.[129]

Baring-Gould interviewed singers at a time when they were waning in popularity. An account written a decade earlier of a fete in Washford Pyne suggests this:

> An itinerant songster paraded the ground and sung the praises of his
> grandmother's armchair but whether it is that armchairs are plentiful or cash
> scarce, his love ditties and armchair ballads got few customers.[130]

Undated photograph of Robert Hard of Ugborough, ballad singer.

One of Baring-Gould's singers was Jim Parsons, an agricultural labourer, hedger and thatcher, who was known as the Singing Machine. His father and grandfather had also been ballad singers and he, his wife and parents had sung in harmony at village events and at crossroads.

Adam Laundry, then seventy-seven years old, was another of these men. Baring-Gould later recollected meeting Laundry in North Hill in Cornwall:

> I found him cutting ferns in a field. I asked him if he knew *The Oxen*
> *Ploughing.* He did. So I sat on a heap of cut fern and he on another and he
> sang it, and I after him, till I had got it by heart. All the way home, a drive of
> eighteen miles, I continued singing it till I reached Lew [Trenchard] and was
> able to note it down with the aid of my piano.[131]

Another singer was Ginger Jack, 'a small dwarfish man', properly known as John Woodridge or even John Woodrich. His father and grandfather had also been ballad singers. Woodridge had been born in Somerset and moved to Lew Trenchard. During his lifetime he worked as a blacksmith, navvy and labourer. Of one song he had:

> heard this recited and sung in 1874 near Bideford by a very old man in a
> public house who, as he said and sang it, stood bent leaning on his staff that
> shook with him under the palsy of old age. This old man did not know all the
> verses and recited where he had forgotten.

Of another he said:

> This was sung by a woman – she was so drunk that she couldn't sing more
> than these two verses and she sung 'em over and over – that there was no
> forgetting 'em.[132]

A South Brent dentist introduced two singers to Baring-Gould who later recollected:

> My host who had invited me, had invited neighbours to dinner to meet me;
> and after dinner the entire party adjourned to the roomy, warm and pleasant
> kitchen, where we found the miller and the stonebreaker, and the wife of the

former in an old white mob-cap. They were seated by the fire, with a table before them on which stood grog. The servants of the house sat along one side of the kitchen, the guests on the other.

He had misgivings, which proved to be well founded.

> I was not at all sure that the words of the ballads would in all cases be fit for ladies' ears. And so it proved. For after the singing of *The Mole Catcher* by John Helmore, the aged miller, there ensued a rapid dissolution of the company. I inserted the song in the last edition of *Songs of the West*, but to very much chastened words.

On another occasion Lifton's rector collected the saucy lyrics while Baring-Gould noted the melody. When the words were later read it was apparent that the firm hand, which was apparent at the start, had been replaced by increasingly shaky writing. The final stanzas were illegible.[133]

Baring-Gould concluded that:

> Some of the earliest and boldest airs are associated to very objectionable words… some wild and rugged moor men are very bad, yet the airs are splendid.

He rewrote ballads he considered indelicate or obscene by substituting verses in order for them 'to be sung in a drawing room'.[134]

He was conscious of this with one particular singer of 'Widdicombe Fair'. Baring-Gould recalled:

> One day I was at Belstone visiting a famous singer, Harry Westaway, when he sang a ballad to us, but dropped one of the verses whereupon his daughter, a tall handsome girl of about eighteen, shouted from the kitchen, *Fayther you've left out someut* and she stuck up and sang a most – to say the least – indelicate verse.[135]

The sanitation of these ballads helped ensure their acceptance by the middle class who subsequently adopted many of them, including 'Widdicombe Fair', for performing at public events such as church fundraising. It would have been unthinkable to sing their coarser versions.

'Widdicombe Fair' before 1889

Until its publication the public had, for generations, learned the ballad aurally and this encouraged occasional if not continual changes according to the whim of the singer. Harry Westaway's variants sung in 1941 and 1950 demonstrate how the song could alter. (Versions 2a-b) Just as different is the truncated version of 'Widdicombe Fair' performed by Charles Tree, a well-known Edwardian baritone,' in 1915.[136] Publication also fixed the ballad's title. Until then it had been known under various names but never as 'Widdicombe Fair'. At Slapton and in London in 1889 it was performed as 'Uncle Tom Cobley'. Before this, in 1875, it was sung as 'Uncle Tom Cobley and I' at Tewkesbury. The latter was an amateur performance at the music hall. It was reported:

Detail of Dartmouth, by John Baverstock Knight, 1823.

> Mr Pearce [was] in the garb of a countryman, the character being most
> complete. He sang *The Turmut Hoer* and in response to an encore changed
> his appearance a little and gave *Uncle Tom Cobley and I*. A fund of merriment
> was caused by the clever style in which Mr Pearce acquitted himself of this
> innocent bit of fun, and very hearty expressions of applause were elicited.[137]

Other earlier titles were also recorded: in 1878 at South Molton it was 'Sam Pearce's
Mare' while seven years earlier in Dartmouth it was 'Old Uncle Tom Cobley and All'
and earlier another Dartmouth audience danced to the fore-mentioned 'Uncle Tom
Cobley's Quadrille'.[138]

Until 1889 the ballad had another more common association. In Hastings in 1874 it
was called 'Tom Pierce'[139] as it was in London in 1885. Another variant, 'Tom Pearce's
Grey Mare', was heard at Chard in 1852[140] but in the 1880s at Horsham, Northampton,
Buckingham, Leiston near Ipswich, Horsham and Daventry it was known as 'Tom
Pearse's Old Mare'.[141]

Even after the publication of 'Widdicombe Fair' the ballad had other titles. In the
1890s 'Father, Tom Cobleigh and I' was performed at Winchester, 'Uncle Tom Cobley'
was heard in Wiveliscombe and Brightling, 'Tom Pearse's Grey Mare' was heard in
Arlington and Chard, and 'Tom Pearse's Old Mare' was sung in Oxfordshire. No doubt
many other such performances were unrecorded.[142]

The number of performances across England raises the question as to whether
the ballad originated in Devon. In 1895 it was recalled that farmers at Flixton in
Cheshire had commonly sung 'a version of that very droll song known in Devonshire
as Widdicombe Fair'.[143] It is unclear if the ballad had a different name in Cheshire.

The uncertainty of the song's origins had greeted its publication in 1889. In various
places across England it was viewed as 'the famous Devonshire song' (Aldermaston),
'the amusing old Devonshire ditty' (Penzance), 'the quaint and humorous old
Devonshire song' (St Breward, Cornwall) 'an old Devonshire song which dates back
five centuries' (Bolton) and 'an old Devon folk song of great quaintness and much
drollness of character' (Kenilworth).[144] On at least three occasions, in Nutfield
in Surrey, at Eastbourne and in Colwall in Worcestershire, it was recorded as a
Somerset song.[145] A publication subsequent to *Songs of the West* had questioned the
origins of 'Widdicombe Fair': in it Cecil Sharp suggested that it was originally from
Somerset.[146] Its existence in that county before the publication of 'Widdicombe Fair'
is demonstrated by a Somerset dialect book in 1877. The author noted 'a well-known

song has the chorus refrain ending in '*Un poo·ŭr oa·l uung·kl Tau·m Kaub·lĕe un aw·l*' which was 'poor old Uncle Tom Cobley and all'.[147] However, in 1950 Hamlyn Parsons, then the Devonshire Association's Recorder of Verbal Provincialisms, disputed Sharp's claims. He wrote Sharp had:

> a tendency to call everything he first heard there *Somerset*. We later had our
> county's folk song ('Widdicombe Fair') dubbed Somerset just because he
> found a polyglot thing derived there from somewhere round Exmoor. A song
> starts in one particular place, with particular references, only when it has
> spread further afield does it become generalised.

Parsons was in communication with Peter Kennedy, a song collector, who had repeated Sharp's view by suggesting 'Widdicombe Fair' had merely been adapted in Devon.[148] More than a decade later, in 1967, Kenneth Williams's version indicated the ballad was from Somerset. (Version 52)

Cornwall has also laid claim. A Cornishman wrote that he had heard it in the 1830s[149] and Tom Pearce was a character in a traditional Cornish Christmas play in which a performer, upon seeing a corpse, says:

> Ashes to ashes, dust to dust
> If Uncle Tom Pearce won't have him, Aunt Molly must.[150]

The ballad was sung by another name ('Helston Fair') as early as 1878[151] and in 1913 Cornish lyrics were suggested:

> Tom Peerce, Tom Peerce, lend me your grey maare, fur I want fur to go to
> Widdicombe Fear, weth Bill Brewer, Jan Stewer, Peteh Gurney, Dicky Boo,
> Dan'l Widden, Josey Paull, Harry Hawke, and Uncle Tom Cobleigh an awl, an
> Uncle Tom Cobleigh and awl.[152]

A Cornish collector of songs wrote that an elderly Cornish woman told him that 'her mother knew Tom Pearce who lived at Truro and loaned the grey mare to go to Summercourt Fair.' In Looe in 1891 the ballad was called 'Tam Pearce's Grey Mare'.[153]

Baring-Gould believed that the ballad had its origins in the eighteenth century but could find no supporting evidence. However, a single copy of an Exeter electoral ballad

Old Uncle Tom Cobley and All

Four illustrations produced in Widecombe for the souvenier trade, mid twentieth century.

Tom Pearce's Old Mare, er took zick and er died

That aint the end of the shocking affair

Tom Pearce's Old Mare appears ghastly white

has survived from 1761. This broadsheet had the tune 'Old Cobley' and was highly derogatory about opposition politicians: one local man was termed Lord Petulant Flat. The earliest recollection was that of Miss F. J. Adams who remembered her mother singing it in Kingsbridge in 1822.[154]

Other versions

Nearly sixty complete versions of 'Widdicombe Fair' have been identified as well as a considerable number of fragments.[155] The complete variants form the Appendices. There has been no attempt made by the author to identify those variants sung in the British Empire and in other English speaking nations.[156]

There are twelve traditional variants for Devon. One predates 'Widdicombe Fair' by twenty-two years but the majority are either of the same date (three are of 1888–9) or later (between 1903 and c1960). Baring-Gould had two alternative variants. His printed version comprised eight verses, included seven excursionists and the well known chorus of 'all along, down along, out along lea' and identified the mare's owner as Tom Pierce. There is at least one difference between each of the other variants. Some of these are marked including the omission of Peter Gurney from the company. In total the fourteen variants run to between four and ten verses. Baring-Gould himself used different titles in his manuscript and subsequent printed editions (one is called 'Tom Pearce, Tom Pearce') and the other variants had names such as 'Tom Pearce's Grey Mare', 'Old Uncle Tom Cobley' and 'Uncle Tom Cobley & All'.

There were also changes in the chorus. 'Widdicombe Fair' began with two lines:

> 'Tom Pearse, Tom Pearse, lend me your grey mare,
>> All along, down along, out along, lee.'

This second line was substituted in the other verses by six other lines:

> 'all along, all along, all along lea',
> 'all along, out along, up along',
> 'an-to-be-lone, a lallee-lal-lee',
> 'al along, al along lane an a lee',
> 'hey along, ding along, ding',
> and surprisingly,
> 'ri-fol-diddle-ol, diddle-I-do' and 'ri-fol lol-the-dol diddle-i-do.

Study in watercolour, pen and brown ink entitled *A quarry near Widecombe*, by John White Abbott, 1792. Its precise location is uncertain.

The phrase 'up along', recorded in the Kingsbridge variant in 1889 (Version 5), was then used in Devon to mean 'uphill' or 'towards home'. In North Devon it is more closely connected with Clovelly where its main street is known as Up Along or Down Along.[157] In 1900 in Devon the word 'along' was 'very commonly used as a sort of complement or frequentative without adding anything to the meaning'.[158]

'Widdicombe Fair' tells the story in eight verses:

1. An unknown person asks to borrow Tom Pearce's mare to travel to Widecombe Fair.
2. A promise is made that she will be returned by Saturday mid day.
3. The mare is not returned.
4. Tom Pearce finds the horse dying.
5. The mare dies and Pearce cries.
6. The saga continues.
7. The mare's ghost periodically appears on the moor.
8. Noises are heard from the dead mare.

In 1891 Baring-Gould admitted he omitted one verse because there was a lack of space but his notes show he had two more than in the printed version.[159] One of these was Verse Five:

> And how did he know that it was his grey mare?
> All along, down along, out along lee
> 'Cos one foot was shoed, & the to'ther was bare.

This also appeared in variants collected at Colebrooke, Feniton, Kingsbridge and Torquay at around the same time as well as in Somerset in 1904. This verse was also included in versions later sung by the son of Harry Westaway.

Secondly, Baring-Gould also omitted a verse about the mare's burial. (Version 1c)

> And now that Tom Pearse's old grey mare is dead
> All along, down along, out along lee
> They all did agree that her should be buried.

This was also included in contemporary variants from Torquay and Kingsbridge. (Versions 4 & 5) It appears as though Baring-Gould's truncated version was not representative.

Edward Dunn, who impersonated Cobley at Widecombe Fair and claimed to be his direct descendant, asserted in 1934 that he had found another missing verse in a family bible. He performed it that year at the fair.

> And they all walked home from Widecombe Fair
> > All along, down along, out along lee
> Though they buried the other they bought Tom Pearce another
> > Did Bill Brewer, Jan Stewer, Peter Gurney,
> Peter Davy, Dan'l Whidden, Harry Hawke,
> > Old Uncle Tom Cobley and all
> > Old Uncle Tom Cobley and all.[160]

However, this bible has yet to be found.

Eight versions altered the order of the verses or are composites. In some variants the mare's appearance at night was put at midnight, in some it was the bones of the riders that were rattled, and in one instance the mare's grave was identified as being on top of a hill. The variants from Berkshire and Sussex differ most from Baring-Gould's version.(Versions 11 & 15)

The company of excursionists considerably altered in their number and constituents; they ranged from none to thirteen. The unidentified narrator needs to be included as well. The number even differed in Baring-Gould's own three versions of 'Widdicombe Fair'. No women were mentioned except in a version to Tavistock Fair where the company included Miss Brewer, Cherry Bine and Ivy Bowen.[161] The most famous of them, Tom Cobley, appears in nearly all, mostly with the prefix 'Uncle', but in one he was substituted by 'Tom Cockerel'. There are other instances of his name being altered to Your Uncle Tom Cobber (Bedford), Uncle Tom Goblin (Wiltshire), Uncle Tom Coblin (Somerset) and Uncle Tom Cobble (Cornwall).[162] In Hampshire and Cornwall he was called Uncle Joe Maybe.[163] In all the variants Tom Pearce was nearly always named as the mare's owner although in Sussex he was not Tom (or Tam) but Gaffer Pearce.[164]

Baring-Gould cited six or seven excursionists in his versions of 'Widdicombe Fair'. They comprised Bill Brewer, Jan Stewer, Peter Davy, Daniel Whiddon, Harry Hawk,

Uncle Tom Cobley and sometimes Peter Gurney. It has been suggested that all these men resided in or near Spreyton or Sticklepath[165] but these names differed with each variant. Some were retained and others were cut. As noted earlier, the inclusion of local figures was one reason for its popularity and this may have been the case in Feniton in 1867. That version also features local surnames that suggests that those mentioned were also probably known individuals. It is likely that this also applied to the men cited in the lyrics for the Belstone, Colebrooke, Harberton, Kingsbridge and Torquay variants.

The first two surnames in 'Widecombe Fair' appear to be included because they rhymed but their names (Bill Brewer, Jan Stewer) altered in other variants (including Will Lewer, Jan Stewer; Will Brewer, Jan Stewer; Tom Lewer, Will Brewer; Bill Brewer, Jack Stewer). The other four men were often included in the variants but also appeared differently:

> Peter Gurney was also Peter Guernsey and Dick Guernsey
>
> Peter Davy became Joe Davy and Dick Davy
>
> Daniel Whiddon was David Witten and David Whiddon
>
> Harry Hawke was also Harry Hawkins and Harry Hawker

Many other names were sung and their musicality was probably responsible for their inclusion; for instance, Tom Kemp, Tom Dyer, Tom Toad and Tom Duke in one instance and Clark Higgins and Giles Wiggins in another. 'Stumpy the Weaver' may have been liked because his was a comical name while in that same list 'the pot-bellied Gale' easily rhymed with 'Wale'.

Fair and cumulative fair songs

The fair at Widecombe-in-the-Moor began in 1850 which would mean that earlier versions of the ballad had to cite another fair. This contradicts a tale that the song is based on an excursion to Widecombe in September 1802.[166] It should also be noted that the choice of Widecombe-in-the-Moor as the destination was not just sung north of the moor; it was also used in the Kingsbridge variant published a few months earlier than that by Baring-Gould. In the Feniton version the fair took place at Hoodycock, the Devon dialect word for a woodcock or for a 'particular kind of unproductive soil'.[167] In the 1920s J. F. Chanter observed that variants collected earlier than those by

Baring-Gould had the fair at 'Hoodicot'.[168] In 1888 T. C. Down of Plymouth also had a version which he called 'Tam Pearse' or 'Tam Pearce's Ole Mare'. This also echoed that of Feniton:

> Tam Pearce he goes up 'pintap Oodycock Hill
> An a sees his ole mare there amaking hur will[169]

Hoodycock might have been a fictitious, or merely comical, placename.

It is likely that the destination altered according to the whim of the singer. S. T. Rowe of Redruth collected another short variant in 1888. He recalled it from his boyhood in the 1830s:

> Tom Pearce, Tom Pearce, lend me your old mare
> > To ride with Aunt Mary to Tavistock Fair
> With Will Hewer, Jem Brewer and old Jerry Jones, Dick Dibble, Sam Gribble and
> > Uncle Tom Cobble and all.[170]

A second version differed:

> Tom Pearce, Tom Pearce, will you lend me your mare
> > All along, all along, lee
> I want to ride over to Tavistock Fair
> > To my lover Miss Brewer, Dick Mine, Cherry Bine, Will Owen, Joe Bowen,
> > > Sam Gribble, Dick Tibble, Dick Drogy, Uncle Tom C. and all.[171]

In 1899 there was also a North Devon variant. Members of the Folk Song Society heard 'Barnstaple Fair' from Reverend C. F. Chorley Loveband, vicar of West Down. He had been the cleric at South Molton where it had been sung by his grandfather.[172] In 1932 what appears to have been a modern version of 'Honiton Fair' was sung in a concert in East Devon.[173]

There are Cornish versions that refer to fairs at Summercourt by 1929 and Helston as early as 1878. In the latter there is a verse 'Uncle Joe Maybe lent me his old mare'. This was the same name as was recorded in Hampshire in 1907.[174] There are other variants across England including Somerset in 1904 and the 1950s ('Midsummer Fair', 'Lansdown Fair'), Bedford in 1960 ('Bedford Fair'), Gloucester in 1928 ('Stow Fair'),

Detail of a view of Dartmoor by Joseph Mallord William Turner, *c*1813.

Hampshire in 1908 and 1907 ('Illsdown Fair', 'Portsdown Fair') and Sussex in 1931 ('Ashburnham Fair').[175]

A more intriguing citing of 'Chidley' Fair might have been a reference to the town of Chudleigh in Devon. A Victorian nursery rhyme has the verses:

> Driddlety drum, driddety drum
> There you see the beggars are come
> Some are here, and some are there
> And some are gone to Chidley Fair.[176]

This relates to the comical nature of the chorus names. These echo the cumulative fair songs which featured a long list of beggars' names. (Versions 20 to 22) 'Jolly Companions', otherwise known as 'Widlicombe Fair', ends with a chorus giving an extensive list of individuals:

> Then were was Nuts, Old Mother Funny-nuts
> Pots, Old Mother Slobber-chops
> Shake, Old Mother Shake-a-leg
> Yarn, Old Mother Balls of Yarn
> Pins, Old Mother Pricklepins
> Dicks, Old Mother Fiddle-Sticks
> Wax, Old Mother Balls o' Wax
> Balls, Old Mother Bags o' Balls
> Johnny Jumping Joan
> Jolly Companions everyone.[177]

Parodies

Other variants were written to support the war effort from 1914 to 1918 and again from 1939 to 1945, to advertise products and to endorse political candidates. (Versions 23-42) The ballad's popularity encouraged a considerable number of writers to compose their own versions. In 1933 it was lampooned as a gramophone record of which 'the needle keeps getting stuck in one groove'.

Tom Pearse, Tom Pearse, lend me your grey mare
(All along, down along, out along, by-with-or-from-along lea)
For I want for to go, for to Widdicombe Fair
    With Bill Brewer, Bill Brewer, Bill Brewer, Bill Brewer, Bill Brewer, Bill Brewer,
        Bill Brewer… (*Give the needle a shove*)
    Old oblong old Cobley and all
    Old wobbly old Cobley and all.

And when shall I see again my grey mare?
(All along, come along, cut along, get along for Heaven's sake)
    With Bill Bobbly, Will Wobbly, Dick Nobbly, Harry Tate,
Sir John Simon, Sir Pundit Motilal Tej Bahadur, Bahadur, Bahadur, Bahadur,
        Bahadur, Bahadur… (*Another little shove*)
    Old Coblywob-nobly and all
    Hobgobly-nobwobly and all.

Widecombe by John Linnell, mid to late nineteenth century.

Chorus: With Bill Bobbly, Bill Bobbly, Bill Bobbly, Bill Bobbly, Bill Bobbly,
    Bill Bobbly, Bill Bobbly
(O, take the thing right off).[178]

The popularity has led to numerous spoofs including one in the Benny Hill Show in 1973. An unusually comic version had been aired six years earlier by Kenneth Williams. His innuendo-laden 'The Terrible Tale of the Somerset Nog' was part of a skit on the BBC radio programme *Round the Horne*. (Version 52) At about this time Ken Dodd issued his own parody; in 'Diddycombe Fair' Tom Cobley was replaced by 'Dodgy Doddy'.[179]

Conclusion

'Widdicombe Fair' was sung much earlier, in a greater number of counties and in a far wider range of forms than has been previously realised. It has also had many titles and there have been marked differences in the lyrics and the names of each excursionist as well as of those of Tom Cobley and Tom Pearce. The initial enthusiasm of audiences in 1889 has continued and it is intriguing to think that Cobley links publications such as *Workers' Liberty, Personal Computer News, Doctor Who Magazine, Sports Illustrated, Fortean Times, Practical Wireless, Australian Women's Weekly, Radio Communication, National Geographic, The Hollywood Reporter, The Entomologist's Record, Motion Picture Exhibitor, Flight International Magazine, Smash Hits, The Chemist & Druggist* and *The Jerusalem Post Magazine*.[180] Journalists and fiction writers also continue to reference Cobley.

In order to grasp the enduring popularity one only needs to observe the keenness with which modern audiences continue to sing the chorus and their delight when local figures are substituted for the mare's companions. This appeal is also demonstrated by the cumulative fair songs which show how 'Widdicombe Fair' was similar to another song tradition.

The association of Widecombe-in-the-Moor with the ballad predates 'Widdicombe Fair' by a generation but it was not the original destination of Tom Pearce's mare. Other versions of the song cited nearly a dozen other English fairs across England in the nineteenth century. In addition, the men travelled to 'Hoodycock Fair ', a nonsensical event, possibly even earlier. It was Baring-Gould who firmly linked the ballad with a village situated in an appealing and atmospheric location. This increased the ballad's popularity.

It is impossible to identify the original Tom Cobley. There are many candidates, in Devon and elsewhere, but the evidence is insufficient to determine categorically who he was or where he lived. There are also variations in how the men travelled to the fair; Baring-Gould's versions suggest the men rode the mare but other lyrics are ambiguous and in one variant a cart was used.

Parodies were written decades before 'Widdicombe Fair' was published and many others have appeared down to the modern day. They demonstrate an enduring public familiarity and popularity. The translations into foreign languages are a reminder of the appeal far beyond Devon. It must be stressed that this collection is far from complete: there must have been scores of other versions sung over the generations and no doubt some of these will now surface.

For more than a century 'Widdicombe Fair' has been an iconic part of Devon's heritage; it has established itself amongst the rich diversity of the county's identity alongside Sir Walter Ralegh and Sir Francis Drake, clotted cream, Dartmoor's tors, Honiton lace, Agatha Christie, Exeter Cathedral, Braunton Great Field, tin mining, Beryl Cook, cob cottages, the Hoe, the black swans of Dawlish, hedges, the three hares, Torbay palms, *The Hound of the Baskervilles*, Stannary Parliaments, St Boniface, cider, Axminster carpets, Tiverton lace, church bench ends, Clovelly donkeys, Tom Putt apples and Uncle Tom Cobleigh and all.

APPENDICES

The Songs

Nearly sixty permutations of the ballad have been identified. Some are variants of the traditional ballad and others are similar in that they were 'fair songs' with composite lyrics. Three cumulative fair songs have been included in the pages below as comparative ballads. The popularity of 'Widdicombe Fair' also led to many copies and parodies which are also below.

TRADITIONAL

Twenty-three 'traditional' versions of 'Widdicombe Fair' were collected between 1867 and 1960. Eight share the same name but others were called 'Tom Pearse, Tom Pearse', 'Tom Pearce's Grey Mare', 'Tam Pearce', 'Uncle Tom Cobley', 'Old Uncle Tom Cobleigh' and 'Uncle Tam Cobley and All'. Others were named after fairs (Barnstaple, Bedford, Helston, Illsdown, Lansdown, Midsummer, Portsdown and Stow). Only fourteen were collected in Devon. These vary in the number of verses; there are between four and ten. Not all have the refrain 'all along, down along, out along lea' nor do they all include the names of the company which alter from one version to the next. All but one share the same opening verse although many vary in their precise wording. The individuals who collected them included a journalist, head master, commercial traveller, merchant, engineering clerk and several solicitors and musicians. Three had active interests in Dartmoor (William Collier, Hamlyn Parsons, Douglas St Leger Gordon).

VERSIONS 1a-c

Three versions originated with William Frederick Collier but it is not known where he had heard the ballad sung. His family and business connections indicate his natural orbit was Plymouth and the edge of Dartmoor near Yelverton. Collier was a wine and spirit merchant who came from a Quaker background. He was born in 1824 in Old Town Street in Plymouth. The family subsequently moved to Horrabridge and Collier later purchased Woodtown which lay nearby in Whitchurch. He was a founder of Plymouth High School and his brother and father were Liberal Party MPs for Plymouth. Collier was aged 64 when he wrote to Baring-Gould and died thirteen years later in 1902. He had an interest in Devon dialect and recorded several local songs in a book on a Cornish humourist. His mother Emma (Porrett) was from North Hill in Plymouth and his wife Cycill Calmady, although born in London, was raised in Wembury six miles southeast of Plymouth.[181] It would seem logical that Collier's familiarity with the song came from the southwest corner of Devon.

Collier sent his verses in July or September 1888 to Baring-Gould following the famous dinner at which the song-collecting enterprise had begun. The latter published it the following year in his *Songs and Ballads of the West; Folk Songs of Devon & Cornwall Collected from the Mouths of the People*. Baring-Gould explained 'there is one more verse in the original which I have been forced to omit from lack of room'.[182] The book was republished in 1892 as *Songs of the West* and in revised editions in 1905 and 1913.

The first version (1a) has eight verses and became the standard form of the ballad. It was repeatedly reprinted under its misspelled title of *Widdicombe* (instead of Widecombe). There are numerous inconsistencies in the spelling and words of the initial printed editions. The original publication recorded the ballad as both 'Widdicombe Fair' and 'Widdecombe Fair'. In 1905 Sharp used 'Widdecombe Fair' and changed the spelling of Cobbleigh to Cobbley and Pearse to Pearce. The musical arrangement by Reverend Sheppard in his printed edition of 1889 differed from the lyrics in the spelling of two personal names: Cobley was used instead of Cobbleigh while Pearse became Pearce. Baring-Gould's manuscript version in *Songs and Ballads of the West* also has slight changes to the words.[183] In 1907 a Devon reviewer 'hardly recognised' the modernised titles of 'Tam Pearse' and 'Widecombe Vair'.[184]

The second and third variants were written in 1888. The second version (1b) has eight verses and was recorded in Baring-Gould's Plymouth Notebook. He noted that the song was 'well known from Sticklepath down to Tavistock. The names in it are of Sticklepath men. Words & tune traditional'. It differs from his printed version not only in the title ('Tom Pearse, Tom Pearse') but also in the fact that the verses have different spellings and there are additions and omissions of many words including the absence of Peter Gurney from the list of excursionists.

The third (1c) has a different title ('Widdecombe Fair') and also differs from the printed version not just in the wording but also in having two additional verses: in Verse 5 Pearce identified his mare from it having one foot shod and in Verse 7 the company agreed to the mare's burial.[185]

VERSION 1a
'Widdicombe Fair', 1889

1

Tom Pearse, Tom Pearse, lend me your grey mare
    All along, down along, out along, lee
For I want for to go to Widdecombe Fair
    Wi' Bill Brewer, Jan Stewer, Peter Gurney, Peter Davy, Dan'l Whiddon,
Harry Hawk, old Uncle Tom Cobbleigh and all
    CHORUS Old Uncle Tom Cobbleigh and all.

2

And when shall I see again my grey mare?
    All along, down along, out along lee
By Friday soon, or Saturday noon
    With Bill Brewer, Jan Stewer, Peter Gurney, Peter Davy, Dan'l Whiddon,
Harry Hawke, old Uncle Tom Cobbleigh and all
    CHORUS Old Uncle Tom Cobbleigh and all.

3

Then Friday came, and Saturday noon
    All along, down along, out along lee
But Tom Pearce's old mare hath not trotted home
    Wi' Bill Brewer, Jan Stewer, Peter Gurney, Peter Davy, Dan'l Whiddon, Harry
Hawk, old Uncle Tom Cobbleigh and all
    CHORUS Old Uncle Tom Cobbleigh and all.

4

So Tom Pearce he got up to the top o' the hill
  All along, down along, out along lee
And he seed his old mare down a-making her will
  Wi' Bill Brewer, Jan Stewer, Peter Gurney, Peter Davy, Dan'l Whiddon,
Harry Hawk, old Uncle Tom Cobbleigh and all
  CHORUS Old Uncle Tom Cobbleigh and all.

5

So Tom Pearse's old mare, her took sick and died
  All along, down along, out along lee
And Tom he sat down on a stone, and he cried
  Wi' Bill Brewer, Jan Stewer, Peter Gurney, Peter Davy, Dan'l Whiddon,
Harry Hawk, old Uncle Tom Cobbleigh and all
  CHORUS Old Uncle Tom Cobbleigh and all.

6

But this isn't the end o' this shocking affair
  All along, down along, out along lee
Nor, though they be dead, of the horrid career
  Of Bill Brewer, Jan Stewer, Peter Gurney, Peter Davy, Dan'l Whiddon,
Harry Hawk, old Uncle Tom Cobbleigh and all
  CHORUS Old Uncle Tom Cobbleigh and all.

7

When the wind whistles cold on the moor of a night,
  All along, down along, out along lee
Tom Pearse's old mare doth appear gashly white
  Wi' Bill Brewer, Jan Stewer, Peter Gurney, Peter Davy, Dan'l Whiddon,
Harry Hawk, old Uncle Tom Cobbleigh and all
  CHORUS Old Uncle Tom Cobbleigh and all.

8

And all the long night be heard skirling and groans
    All along, down along, out along lee
From Tom Pearce's old mare in her rattling bones
    And from Bill Brewer, Jan Stewer, Peter Gurney, Peter Davy, Dan'l Whiddon,
Harry Hawk, old Uncle Tom Cobbleigh and all
    CHORUS Old Uncle Tom Cobbleigh and all.

VERSION 1b
'Tom Pearse, Tom Pearse', 1888

1

Tom Pearse, Tom Pearse, lend me your grey mare
    All along, down along, out along lee
For I want vor to go to Widdicombe Vair
    Wi' Bill Brewer, Jan Stewer, Peter Davey, Dan'el Widdon, Harry Hawke,
old uncle Tom Cobbly & all
    CHORUS old uncle Tom Cobbly & all.

2

And when shall I zee my old grey mare again?
    All along, down along, out along lee
By Friday zoon, or Zaturday noon
    Wi' Bill Brewer, Jan Stewer, Peter Davey, Dan'el Widdon, Harry Hawke,
old uncle Tom Cobbly & all
    CHORUS old uncle Tom Cobbly & all.

3

Then Vriday came, & Zaturday noon
    All along, down along, out along lee
But Tom Pierce's old mare, her hath not trotted home
    Wi' Bill Brewer, Jan Stewer, Peter Davey, Dan'el Widdon, Harry Hawke,
old uncle Tom Cobbly & all
    CHORUS old uncle Tom Cobbly & all.

4

Zo Tom Pierce he wen on to top o' the hill
　All along, down along, out along lee
And he zeed his old mare down a' making her will
　Wi' Bill Brewer, Jan Stewer, Peter Davey, Dan'el Widdon, Harry Hawke,
old uncle Tom Cobbly & all
　CHORUS old uncle Tom Cobbly & all.

5

Zo Tom Pierce's old mare, her took all zick & died
　All along, down along, out along lee
And Tom Pierce he set down & he bitterly cried
　Wi' Bill Brewer, Jan Stewer, Peter Davey, Dan'el Widdon, Harry Hawke,
old uncle Tom Cobbly & all
　CHORUS old uncle Tom Cobbly & all.

6

But thes isn't the end o' this shocking avair
　All along, down along, out along lee
Nor, though they be dead, o' the horrid career
　Of Bill Brewer, Jan Stewer, Peter Davey, Dan'el Widdon, Harry Hawke,
old uncle Tom Cobbly & all
　CHORUS old uncle Tom Cobbly & all.

7

When the wind, he blows cold, on the moor of a night
　All along, down along, out along lee
Tom Pierce's old mare doth appear, horrid sight
　Wi' Bill Brewer, Jan Stewer, Peter Davey, Dan'el Widdon, Harry Hawke,
old uncle Tom Cobbly & all
　CHORUS old uncle Tom Cobbly & all.

8

And all the long night be heard skirling & groans
　All along, down along, out along lee

From Tom Pierce's old mare in her rattling bones

 From Bill Brewer, Jan Stewer, Peter Davey, Dan'el Widdon, Harry Hawke,
old uncle Tom Cobbly & all

 CHORUS old uncle Tom Cobbly & all.

VERSION 1c
'Widdecombe Fair', 1888

1

Tom Pearse, Tom Pearse, lend me your grey mare

 All along, down along, out along lee

For I wants fer to ride to Widdecombe Fair

 Wi' Bill Brewer, Jan Stewer, Peter Gurney,

 Peter Davey, Dan'l Whidden, Harry Hawke

  Old Uncle Tom Cobley & all

  Old Uncle Tom Cobley & all!

2

O when shall I see again my grey mare again?

 All along, down along, out along lee

On Friday noon, or Saturday soon

 Wi' Bill Brewer, Jan Stewer, Peter Gurney,

 Peter Davey, Dan'l Whidden, Harry Hawke

  Old Uncle Tom Cobley & all

  Old Uncle Tom Cobley & all!

3

Then Friday came, & Saturday noon

 All along, down along, out along lee

But Tom Pearse's old mare her hath not trotted home

 Wi' Bill Brewer, Jan Stewer, Peter Gurney,

 Peter Davey, Dan'l Whidden, Harry Hawke

  Old Uncle Tom Cobley & all

  Old Uncle Tom Cobley & all!

4

So Tom Pearce he got up to the top o' the hill
  All along, down along, out along lee
And he seed his old mare down a-making her will
  Wi' Bill Brewer, Jan Stewer, Peter Gurney,
  Peter Davey, Dan'l Whidden, Harry Hawke,
    Old Uncle Tom Cobley & all
    Old Uncle Tom Cobley & all!

5

And how did he know that it was his grey mare?
  All along, down along, out along lee
'Cos one foot was shoed, & the [sic] to'ther was bare
Wi' Bill Brewer, Jan Stewer, Peter Gurney,
  Peter Davey, Dan'l Whidden, Harry Hawke,
    Old Uncle Tom Cobley & all
    Old Uncle Tom Cobley & all!

6

So Tom Pearse's old mare, her took sick & died
  All along, down along, out along lee
And Tom he sat down on a stone & he cried
  Wi' Bill Brewer, Jan Stewer, Peter Gurney,
  Peter Davey, Dan'l Whidden, Harry Hawke,
    Old Uncle Tom Cobley & all
    Old Uncle Tom Cobley & all!

7

And now that Tom Pearse's old grey mare is dead
  All along, down along, out along lee
They all did agree that her should be buried
  Wi' Bill Brewer, Jan Stewer, Peter Gurney,
  Peter Davey, Dan'l Whidden, Harry Hawke,
    Old Uncle Tom Cobley & all
    Old Uncle Tom Cobley & all!

8

But this isn't the end o' this shocking affair
　　All along, down along, out along lee.
Nor, though they be dead, o' the horrid career
　　Of Bill Brewer, Jan Stewer, Peter Gurney,
　　Peter Davey, Dan'l Whidden, Harry Hawke,
　　　　Old Uncle Tom Cobley & all
　　　　Old Uncle Tom Cobley & all!

9

When the wind whistles cold on the moor, of a night
　　All along, down along, out along lee
Tom Pearse's old mare doth appear gashly white
　　Wi' Bill Brewer, Jan Stewer, Peter Gurney,
　　Peter Davey, Dan'l Whidden, Harry Hawke,
　　　　Old Uncle Tom Cobley & all
　　　　Old Uncle Tom Cobley & all!

10

And all the night they be heard skirling & groans
　　All along, down along, out along lee
From Tom Pearse's old mare in her rattling bones
　　Wi' Bill Brewer, Jan Stewer, Peter Gurney,
　　Peter Davey, Dan'l Whidden, Harry Hawke,
　　　　Old Uncle Tom Cobley & all
　　　　Old Uncle Tom Cobley & all!

VERSIONS 2a-c
'Widecombe Fair', 1941–50

These three variants were sung at Belstone by Harry Westaway in 1941 and 1950 (a &
b) and his brother William, known as Bill, in 1950 (c). There are four, five and nine
verses in each respectively. There are also differences in the lyrics and in the names
of the company. Each brother used 'Ri-fol-diddle-ol, diddle-I-do' or 'Ri-fol lol-the-dol
diddle-i-do' instead of Baring-Gould's 'all along, down along, out along, lee'. This was
similar to a refrain sung by their father in about 1890; 'Oh Ri-fol-lavidol diddledi Oh'.

The first variant (a) has five verses and was collected by Douglas St Leger Gordon[186] who lived at Sticklepath and wrote mainly about nature in Devon. He was born in Canada in about 1888 and died in 1970; his gravestone noted he was a 'Chronicler of Dartmoor, Lover of Nature'.[187]

The verses are similar to 'Widdicombe Fair' but this variant omits the remaining three and introduces one of Baring-Gould's two missing verses which he had recorded in manuscript but not published. In 1931 Gordon wrongly suggested 'the stolid Devonian who sold the original copy of *Widecombe Fair* to Mr Baring-Gould... took care to *keep some o' the best verses for hisself*'.[188] In 1941 Harry Westaway was aged about 74, worked as a gardener and domestic worker, and died in 1954.[189]

The second variant (b) has four verses and was recorded by Peter Kennedy and performed by Harry Westaway nine years later in 1950.[190] There is one less verse in this version and the lyrics contain minor differences including a repeat of the second line and the last.

The third variant (c) by William (Bill) Westaway was also collected by Kennedy[191] and includes four verses additional to those sung nine years earlier by his brother Harry. The names of the company differ from all other versions. Bill Westaway was aged about 78 when he performed the ballad.[192] The Westaways' parents were born in about 1824 and 1833 in Belstone and nearby Whiddon Down. Bill Westaway worked as a blacksmith and died in about 1958. An additional factor in the differences between these versions may lie in their transcriptions.

VERSION 2a
'Widecombe Fair', 1941

1

Tom Pearse, Tom Pearse, lend me your grey mare
    That I might ride out to Widecombe Fair
With Will Lewer, Jan Stewer, Harry Hawkins, Joe Davy, Harry Whitpot,
George Parsley, Dick Wills, Tom Cobley and all.

2

When shall I have my old mare home again?
    Ri-fol-diddle-ol, diddle-I-do

A Friday night or a Saturday morn
With Will Lewer, Jan Stewer, Harry Hawkins, Joe Davy, Harry Whitpot,
George Parsley, Dick Wills, Tom Cobley and all.

3

Friday being past, Saturday was come
   Ri-fol-diddle-ol, diddle-I-do
Tom Pearse's old mare has not a come home
With Will Lewer, Jan Stewer, Harry Hawkins, Joe Davy, Harry Whitpot,
George Parsley, Dick Wills, Tom Cobley and all.

4

Tom Pearse went up upon a high hill
   Ri-fol-diddle-ol, diddle-I-do
There he saw his old mare making her will
With Will Lewer, Jan Stewer, Harry Hawkins, Joe Davy, Harry Whitpot,
George Parsley, Dick Wills, Tom Cobley and all.

5

How did you know it was your old mare?
   Ri-fol-diddle-ol, diddle-I-do
'Cos one foot was shoed and the other three bare
With Will Lewer, Jan Stewer, Harry Hawkins, Joe Davy, Harry Whitpot,
George Parsley, Dick Wills, Tom Cobley and all.

VERSION 2b
'Widecombe Fair', 1950

1

Tom Pearse, Tom Pearse, lend me thee old mare
   Ri-fol-diddle-ol, diddle-I-do
That I might ride out to Widecombe Fair
   With Will Lewer, Jan Brewer, Harry Hawkins, Joe Davy, Harry Whitpot,
George Parsley, Dick Wilson, Tom Cobley and all
   Ere is Uncle Tom Cobley and all.

2

O when shall I have my old mare home again?
   Ri-fol-diddle-ol, diddle-I-do
A Friday night or a Saturday morn
   With Will Lewer, Jan Brewer, Harry Hawkins, Joe Davy, Harry Whitpot,
George Parsley, Dick Wilson, Tom Cobley and all
   Ere is Uncle Tom Cobley and all.

3

And Friday being past, and Saturday was gone
   Ri-fol-diddle-ol, diddle-I-do
Tom Pearse's old mare he was not a come home
   With Will Lewer, Jan Brewer, Harry Hawkins, Joe Davy, Harry Whitpot,
George Parsley, Dick Wilson, Tom Cobley and all
   Ere is Uncle Tom Cobley and all.

4

Tom Pearse went up upon a high hill
   Ri-fol-diddle-ol, diddle-I-do
And there he saw his old mare making her will
   With Will Lewer, Jan Brewer, Harry Hawkins, Joe Davy, Harry Whitpot,
George Parsley, Dick Wilson, Tom Cobley and all
   Ere is Uncle Tom Cobley and all.

VERSION 2c
'Widecombe Fair', 1950

1

Tom Pearce, Tom Pearce, lend me your grey mare
   Ri-fol lol-the-dol diddle-i-do
That I might ride out to Widecombe Fair
   With Will 'Ewer, Jan Brewer, Harry 'Awkins, Joe Davey, Philly Widpotts,
George Parsley, Dick Wilsdon, Tom Cobley an' all
   'Ere is Uncle Tom Cobley an' all.

2

O when shall I see my grey mare home again?
  Ri-fol lol-the-dol diddle-i-do
By a Friday night or a Saturday morn
  With Will 'Ewer, Jan Brewer, Harry 'Awkins, Joe Davey, Philly Widpotts,
George Parsley, Dick Wilsdon, Tom Cobley an' all
  'Ere is Uncle Tom Cobley an' all.

3

Then Friday was passed and Saturday was come
  Ri-fol lol-the-dol diddle-i-do
And Tom Pearce's grey mare was not a-come home
  With Will 'Ewer, Jan Brewer, Harry 'Awkins, Joe Davey, Philly Widpotts,
George Parsley, Dick Wilsdon, Tom Cobley an' all
  'Ere is Uncle Tom Cobley an' all.

4

Tom Pearce he went up then on a high hill
  Ri-fol lol-the-dol diddle-i-do
He saw his old mare down a-making her will
  With Will 'Ewer, Jan Brewer, Harry 'Awkins, Joe Davey, Philly Widpotts,
George Parsley, Dick Wilsdon, Tom Cobley an' all
  'Ere is Uncle Tom Cobley an' all.

5

So how do you know it was your old mare?
  Ri-fol lol-the-dol diddle-i-do
For one foot be shoed and the other three bare
  With Will 'Ewer, Jan Brewer, Harry 'Awkins, Joe Davey, Philly Widpotts,
George Parsley, Dick Wilsdon, Tom Cobley an' all
  'Ere is Uncle Tom Cobley an' all.

6

Tom Pearce's old mare she was took sick and died
   Ri-fol lol-the-dol diddle-i-do
Tom Pearce he sat down on the stones and he cried
      With Will 'Ewer, Jan Brewer, Harry 'Awkins, Joe Davey, Philly Widpotts,
George Parsley, Dick Wilsdon, Tom Cobley an' all
      'Ere is Uncle Tom Cobley an' all.

7

When the wind whistled hard on the moor of a night
   Ri-fol lol-the-dol diddle-i-do
Tom Pearce's old mare she appeared ghastly white
      With Will 'Ewer, Jan Brewer, Harry 'Awkins, Joe Davey, Philly Widpotts,
George Parsley, Dick Wilsdon, Tom Cobley an' all
      'Ere is Uncle Tom Cobley an' all.

8

Then all the night long we heard shirklings and groans
   Ri-fol lol-the-dol diddle-i-do
Tom Pearce's old mare she was rattling her bones
      With Will 'Ewer, Jan Brewer, Harry 'Awkins, Joe Davey, Philly Widpotts,
George Parsley, Dick Wilsdon, Tom Cobley an' all
      'Ere is Uncle Tom Cobley an' all.

9

So this is the end of this shocking affair
   Ri-fol lol-the-dol diddle-i-do
I've just given you the career of Tom Pearce's grey mare
      With Will 'Ewer, Jan Brewer, Harry 'Awkins, Joe Davey, Philly Widpotts,
George Parsley, Dick Wilsdon, Tom Cobley an' all
      'Ere is Uncle Tom Cobley an' all.

VERSION 3
'Tom Pearce's Grey Mare', 1888

These five verses were written before the publication of 'Widdicombe Fair'. [193] They were compiled by John Edward Valentine Henwood who sent them to the *Western Morning News* in response to a letter by T. C. Down, a Plymothian, which had appeared the day before. Down had suggested the title was 'Tam Pearce' or 'Tam Pearce's Ole Mare'. He had only one verse:

Tam Pearce he goes up 'pintap 'Oodycock Hill,
An' a sees his ole mare there amakin' hur will,
Way Will Brewer...[194]

Henwood signed his letter from Great Torrington and claimed that this was the 'correct version' of the ballad. It is not clear where he came by this: he was born in about 1853 in Fowey where he was still living in 1891. A commercial traveller, Henwood moved to Barnstaple by 1901 and to Berkshire ten years later.[195]

1

Tom Pearce, Tom Pearce, lend me yer Grey Mare
    All along, all along, all along lee
To take us away to Witticumbe Fair
    With Will Brewer, Jan Stewer, Petter Davy,
    David Witten, Dick Guernsey, Harry Hawke,
    And Uncle Tom Cobley and all
      Uncle Tom Cobley and all.

2

Naw when shall I zee me Grey Mare again
    All along, all along, all along lee
A Vriday noon or a Zaturday soon
    With Will Brewer, Jan Stewer, Petter Davy,
    David Witten, Dick Guernsey, Harry Hawke,
    And Uncle Tom Cobley and all
      Uncle Tom Cobley and all.

3

Now Vriday's agone and Zaturday's come
 All along, all along, all along lee
But Tom Pearce's Grey Mare is not come home
  Neither is Will Brewer, Jan Stewer, Petter Davy,
  David Witten, Dick Guernsey, Harry Hawke,
  And Uncle Tom Cobley and all
   Uncle Tom Cobley and all.

4

Then Tom Pearce he goes 'pon top of the hill
 All along, all along, all along lee
There he zeed his Grey Mare a making her will
  Will Brewer, Jan Stewer, Petter Davy,
  David Witten, Dick Guernsey, Harry Hawke,
  And Uncle Tom Cobley and all
   Uncle Tom Cobley and all.

5

The winds whistled wildly through the depth of the night
 All along, all along, all along lee
When about 12 o'clock there was a more horrid sight
  Of Will Brewer, Jan Stewer, Petter Davy,
  David Witten, Dick Guernsey, Harry Hawke,
  And Uncle Tom Cobley and all
   Uncle Tom Cobley and all.

VERSION 4
'Tam Pearce', 1888

In 1888 Claude R. Fowles wrote from Torquay to the *Western Morning News* to add five verses which he noted were missing from T. C. Down's variant sent two days earlier. Fowles' version changed Daniel Whiddon's first name to David and included Tom Blackworthy as one of the company.[196]

 Fowles was a musician. He was the organist and choirmaster at three Torquay churches and performed at local musical events including singing one song in 1888

Torquay, *c*1880.

entitled 'There was nothing between them'. It is uncertain where Fowles obtained the lyrics. Only ten years earlier he had moved to Torbay from the Isle of Wight where he and his parents were born. Fowles died in early retirement at Yelverton in 1904 at the age of 47.[197] His wife Martha was a Londoner. Fowles appears to have been most familiar with Torbay which, although considerably suburbanised by this period, still had at least one ballad singer: Albert John Dymond, a wandering minstrel who specialised in impromptu songs, attended fairs and regattas from Teignmouth to Paignton.[198]

1

Tam Pearce, Tam Pearce, land us yer Grey Mare
    All along, all along, all along lea
That us may ride over to Widdicombe Fair
    With Bill Brewer, Jan Stewer, Peter Guernsey,
    Peter Davy, David Whiddon, Harry Hawker,
    Tom Blackworthy, and
       Old Uncle Tom Cobley and all.

2

When shall us zee the Grey Mare back agin
    All along, all along, all along lea
On a Vriday noon or Zaturday zoon
     With Bill Brewer, Jan Stewer, Peter Guernsey,
     Peter Davy, David Whiddon, Harry Hawker,
     Tom Blackworthy, and
       Old Uncle Tom Cobley and all.

3

Vriday's gone and Zaturday's come
    All along, all along, all along lea
But Tam Pearce's Grey Mare hur h'arnt a come home
     With Bill Brewer, Jan Stewer, Peter Guernsey,
     Peter Davy, David Whiddon, Harry Hawker,
     Tom Blackworthy, and
       Old Uncle Tom Cobley and all.

4

Tam Pearce he goes 'pon top of the hill
    All along, all along, all along lea
And he zeed his Grey Mare a making hur will
     With Bill Brewer, Jan Stewer, Peter Guernsey,
     Peter Davy, David Whiddon, Harry Hawker,
     Tom Blackworthy, and
       Old Uncle Tom Cobley and all.

5

How ded he know 'twas his Grey Mare
    All along, all along, all along lea
'Cos one fut was shoed and t'other dree bare
     With Bill Brewer, Jan Stewer, Peter Guernsey,
     Peter Davy, David Whiddon, Harry Hawker,
     Tom Blackworthy, and
       Old Uncle Tom Cobley and all.

6

Tam Pearce's Grey Mare took sick and died
    All along, all along, all along lea
And for hur loss he so bitterly cried
    With Bill Brewer, Jan Stewer, Peter Guernsey,
    Peter Davy, David Whiddon, Harry Hawker,
    Tom Blackworthy, and
        Old Uncle Tom Cobley and all.

7

And now that Tam Pearce's Grey Mare is dead
    All along, all along, all along lea
They all agreed hur should be buried
    With Bill Brewer, Jan Stewer, Peter Guernsey,
    Peter Davy, David Whiddon, Harry Hawker,
    Tom Blackworthy, and
        Old Uncle Tom Cobley and all.

8

In the midst of the night us hears screech'us and groans
    All along, all along, all along lea
As the ole Grey, Grey Mare, hur rattles the bones
    Of Bill Brewer, Jan Stewer, Peter Guernsey,
    Peter Davy, David Whiddon, Harry Hawker,
    Tom Blackworthy, and
        Old Uncle Tom Cobley and all.

9

When the wind whistles shrill through the trees of a night
    All along, all along, all along lea
'Zactly at twelve the mare, horrid zite
    With Bill Brewer, Jan Stewer, Peter Guernsey,
    Peter Davy, David Whiddon, Harry Hawker,
    Tom Blackworthy, and
        Old Uncle Tom Cobley and all.

VERSION 5
'Old Uncle Tom Cobley', 1889

In the first weeks of 1889, more than six months before Baring-Gould's 'Widdicombe Fair' was published, William Davies of Kingsbridge compiled the lyrics for 'Old Uncle Tom Cobley' from what were then described as 'various sources'. He also composed the 'symphonies and pianoforte accompaniment'. This variant of the ballad was published by J. R. Gill, music seller and stationer at 101 & 103 Fore Street, Kingsbridge, and described as 'A Devonshire Country Melody'. In 1903 the lyrics were reprinted in *The Sporting Times*.[199] There are nine verses.

Davies, a solicitor, also wrote for *Devon & Cornwall Notes & Queries* and the Devonshire Association.[200] He was born in Exeter in 1843 and was living in Kingsbridge when he wrote the lyrics and composed the music. His wife Elizabeth was born in nearby Malborough. It would be logical to presume that Davies' familiarity with the ballad was due to his connections with the South Hams or Exeter. The story line is similar but not exact to that later published by Baring-Gould. The first two lines and the chorus have broad similarities but Davies' excursionists numbered nine; there is not only Dick (instead of Peter) Davy but two new men in the shape of Tam Ripley and Jack Gribble.

1

Tam Pearce, Tam Pearce, lend us your grey mare
  All along, out along, up along lea
That we may ride to Widdicombe Fair
  With Bill Brewer, Jan Stewer, Peter Gurney, Dick Davy, Dan Whiddon,
Harry Hawker, Tam Ripley, Jack Gribble and old Uncle Tom Cobley and all
  And old Uncle Tom Cobley and all
  And old Uncle Tom Cobley and all.

2

When shall us zee the grey mare back again
  All along, out along, up along lea
On Vriday zoon or Zaturday noon
With Bill Brewer, Jan Stewer, Peter Gurney, Dick Davy, Dan Whiddon,
Harry Hawker, Tam Ripley, Jack Gribble and old Uncle Tom Cobley and all
  And old Uncle Tom Cobley and all
  And old Uncle Tom Cobley and all.

3

Vriday's gone and Zaturday's come
    All along, out along, up along lea
But Tam Pearce's old mare hur harn't a come home
    With Bill Brewer, Jan Stewer, Peter Gurney, Dick Davy, Dan Whiddon,
Harry Hawker, Tam Ripley, Jack Gribble and old Uncle Tom Cobley and all
    And old Uncle Tom Cobley and all
    And old Uncle Tom Cobley and all.

4

Tam Pearce he goes 'pon top of the hill
    All along, out along, up along lea
And he zeed his grey a-making her will
    With Bill Brewer, Jan Stewer, Peter Gurney, Dick Davy, Dan Whiddon,
Harry Hawker, Tam Ripley, Jack Gribble and old Uncle Tom Cobley and all
    And old Uncle Tom Cobley and all
    And old Uncle Tom Cobley and all.

5

How did he know that 'twas hees grey mare
    All along, out along, up along lea
'Cos one foot was shoed and the t'other dree bare
    With Bill Brewer, Jan Stewer, Peter Gurney, Dick Davy, Dan Whiddon,
Harry Hawker, Tam Ripley, Jack Gribble and old Uncle Tom Cobley and all
    And old Uncle Tom Cobley and all
    And old Uncle Tom Cobley and all.

6

Tam Pearce's grey mare hur took zick and died
    All along, out along, up along lea
And fur hur loss he so bitterly cried
    With Bill Brewer, Jan Stewer, Peter Gurney, Dick Davy, Dan Whiddon,
Harry Hawker, Tam Ripley, Jack Gribble and old Uncle Tom Cobley and all
    And old Uncle Tom Cobley and all
    And old Uncle Tom Cobley and all.

7

And now Tam Pearce's grey mare is dead
    All along, out along, up along lea
They all agreed hur should be burryied
    With Bill Brewer, Jan Stewer, Peter Gurney, Dick Davy, Dan Whiddon,
Harry Hawker, Tam Ripley, Jack Gribble and old Uncle Tom Cobley and all
    And old Uncle Tom Cobley and all
    And old Uncle Tom Cobley and all.

8

The wind whistles shrill through the trees of a night
    All along, out along, up along lea
There was zactly at twelve a most horrid sight
    With Bill Brewer, Jan Stewer, Peter Gurney, Dick Davy, Dan Whiddon,
Harry Hawker, Tam Ripley, Jack Gribble and old Uncle Tom Cobley and all
    And old Uncle Tom Cobley and all
    And old Uncle Tom Cobley and all.

9

In the midst of the night us heard screeches and groans
    All along, out along, up along lea
As the old grey mare hur rattled the bones
    Of Bill Brewer, Jan Stewer, Peter Gurney, Dick Davy, Dan Whiddon,
Harry Hawker, Tam Ripley, Jack Gribble and old Uncle Tom Cobley and all
    And old Uncle Tom Cobley and all
    And old Uncle Tom Cobley and all.

VERSION 6
'Widdecombe Fair', 1903

Written in four verses, this variant was sent in 1903 to *The Sporting Times* by 'Pidgon' or 'Pidjon' who explained that he had heard it sung in Colebrooke. He described it as 'an old Devon ballad' and the 'well-known West Country Widdecombe Fair or Uncle John Cobley'.[201] Some of the surnames of the company (Kemp, Perkins) were then to be found in Colebrooke. A resident of nearby Coleford later remembered that Peter Greenslade was sung in preference to Peter Gurney.[202]

1

Tom Pearse, whit thee lend me thee old grey mare
Vor to ride to Widdecombe Fair
  Vor to see Tom Lewer, Will Brewer, Dick Stewer, Phil Wheaton, Harry
Hawkes, Kit Perkins, Harry Lambert, Joe Bradley, Tom Kemp, Tom Dyer,
Tom Toad, Tom Duke,
  And Uncle Tom Cobley and all.

2

Well, if I lend thee me old grey mare
When shall I see her home again?
Why Friday be noon or Saturday soon
  With Tom Lewer, Will Brewer, Dick Stewer, Phil Wheaton, Harry Hawkes,
Kit Perkins, Harry Lambert, Joe Bradley, Tom Kemp, Tom Dyer, Tom Toad,
Tom Duke,
  And Uncle Tom Cobley and all.

3

Why Friday is past and Saturday is come
Yet old Tom Pearse's mare idden come home
  With Tom Lewer, Will Brewer, Dick Stewer, Phil Wheaton, Harry Hawkes,
Kit Perkins, Harry Lambert, Joe Bradley, Tom Kemp, Tom Dyer, Tom Toad,
Tom Duke,
  And Uncle Tom Cobley and all.

4

Tom Pearse he sets forth to seek his old grey mare
And there he sees her coming
When one foot a-shoed and the t'other three bare
  With Tom Lewer, Will Brewer, Dick Stewer, Phil Wheaton, Harry Hawkes,
Kit Perkins, Harry Lambert, Joe Bradley, Tom Kemp, Tom Dyer, Tom Toad,
Tom Duke,
  And Uncle Tom Cobley and all.

VERSION 7
'Uncle Tom Cobleigh' or 'Widdecombe Fair', 1903

George Esmond Adams of Yeoford sent this variant on 20 January 1903 to *The Sporting Times*. He claimed that this was the authentic version. It has five verses. Adams added '*en passant*, may I say that occasionally, in order to introduce local colour to the song, names of the audience are added to or substituted for the set names preceding the penultimate line of chorus'.[203]

Adams was then aged about 28 and was most familiar with the northern edge of Dartmoor where it is likely he heard the ballad. His father, who was the schoolmaster at Yeoford from 1878 to 1912, was born in Plymouth as was his mother. He himself was born in Okehampton in about 1875.[204] The census of 1901 places him in Yeoford.[205]

1

Tom Pearse, Tom Pearse, lain me yur grey mare
    All along, down along, out along, lay
For I want ver go tu Widdicome Vair
    Way Beel Brewer, Jan Stewer, Peter Gurney, Peter Davy, Dan'l Whiddon,
Horry Hawk, Old Uncle Tom Cobleigh and all, Old Uncle Tom Cobleigh
and all
    CHORUS Old Uncle Tom Cobleigh and all
    Old Uncle Tom Cobleigh and all.

2

And whain zhall I zee again my grey mare
    All along, down along, out along, lay
By Vriday soon or Saturday noon
    With Beel Brewer, Jan Stewer, Peter Gurney, Peter Davy, Dan'l Whiddon,
Horry Hawk, Old Uncle Tom Cobleigh and all, Old Uncle Tom Cobleigh
and all
    CHORUS Old Uncle Tom Cobleigh and all
    Old Uncle Tom Cobleigh and all.

3

Then Vriday came, and Zaturday noon
    All along, down along, out along, lay
But Tom Pearse's old mare hathn' tratted home
    With Beel Brewer, Jan Stewer, Peter Gurney, Peter Davy, Dan'l Whiddon,
Horry Hawk, Old Uncle Tom Cobleigh and all, Old Uncle Tom Cobleigh and all
    CHORUS Old Uncle Tom Cobleigh and all
    Old Uncle Tom Cobleigh and all.

4

So Tom Pearse he got up to the top o' the heel
    All along, down along, out along, lay
And he zeed hees old mare down a making her weel
    With Beel Brewer, Jan Stewer, Peter Gurney, Peter Davy, Dan'l Whiddon,
Horry Hawk, Old Uncle Tom Cobleigh and all, Old Uncle Tom Cobleigh and all
    CHORUS Old Uncle Tom Cobleigh and all
Old Uncle Tom Cobleigh and all.

5

So Tom Pearse's old mare her took zick and died
    All along, down along, out along, lay
And Tom he zat down on a stone, and he cried
    With Beel Brewer, Jan Stewer, Peter Gurney, Peter Davy, Dan'l Whiddon,
Horry Hawk, Old Uncle Tom Cobleigh and all, Old Uncle Tom Cobleigh and all
    CHORUS Old Uncle Tom Cobleigh and all
Old Uncle Tom Cobleigh and all.

6

But this idden the aind o' this shocking avair
    All along, down along, out along, lay
Nor, though they be daid, of the horrid career
    Of Bill Brewer, Jan Stewer, Peter Gurney, Peter Davy, Dan'l Whiddon,
Horry Hawk, Old Uncle Tom Cobleigh and all, Old Uncle Tom Cobleigh and all
    CHORUS Old Uncle Tom Cobleigh and all
Old Uncle Tom Cobleigh and all.

7

When the wind whistles cold on moor of a night
    All along, down along, out along, lay
Tom Pearse's old mare doth appear gashly white
    Wi' Brewer, Jan Stewer, Peter Gurney, Peter Davy, Dan'l Whiddon,
Horry Hawk, Old Uncle Tom Cobleigh and all, Old Uncle Tom Cobleigh and all
    CHORUS Old Uncle Tom Cobleigh and all
Old Uncle Tom Cobleigh and all.

8

And all the long night be yeard skirling and groans
    All along, down along, out along, lay
From Tom Pearse's old mare in her rattling bones
    And from Bill Brewer, Jan Stewer, Peter Gurney, Peter Davy, Dan'l Whiddon,
Horry Hawk, Old Uncle Tom Cobleigh and all, Old Uncle Tom Cobleigh and all
    CHORUS Old Uncle Tom Cobleigh and all
Old Uncle Tom Cobleigh and all.

VERSION 8
'Widecombe Fair', 1950

Peter Kennedy of the Dartington Institute of Traditional Arts collected these lyrics and published them in 1971. Kennedy then lived nearby in Harberton. His family background lay in folk songs: Kennedy's father had succeeded Cecil Sharp as director of the English Folk Dance Society and his mother was founding secretary in 1911. He collected folk songs in the West Country from about 1949 and this version was supplied by Hamlyn Parsons the following year. Parsons had recalled the song 'as sung' to him at Harberton near Totnes '30 or 40 years' previously. He also noted the date as being 1913. Parsons wrote to Kennedy that 'there was another verse which I cannot trace now, which is a pity, as when it was collected the old chap did not quite like his questioner, and *kept the best two verses tu mezel*, as he said, so the printed version is a bit truncated.'[206] He was born there in 1909[207] which would have made him too young to remember the lyrics with any accuracy. Parsons became a teacher, was acquainted with A. J. Coles (Jan Stewer) and served as a 'recorder of verbal provincialisms' for the Devonshire Association. His mother was Cornish but Parsons claimed 'I am Devonshire born and bred, on my mother's side of the family I can claim descent from a family which held two manors in Devon at the time of Domesday. Born and bred in a small village, I know the people and the dialect well.' He died in 1961 at Christow where he had been the schoolmaster.[208] The song has five verses. The company includes Bob Paul who was also independently remembered as one of the excursionists by a resident of Exeter in 1948. Of him Parsons wrote 'you will note an extra name – Bob Paul – well, this character figured over quite a large area of Devon. This was made very clear in correspondence in the columns of the *Western Morning News* a couple of years ago and it does rhyme'.[209]

1

Tom Pearce, Tom Pearce, lend me your grey mare
    All-along, down-along, out-along leigh
For I want for to go to Widecombe Fair
    With Bill Brewer, Jan Stewer, Peter Gurney, Peter Davey, Dan'l Whiddon,
Harry Hawke, Bob Paul,
    Old Uncle Tom Cobley and all
    Old Uncle Tom Cobley and all.

2

Tom Pearce's owd mare, she fell sick on the way
    All-along, down-along, out-along leigh
She wouldn't take feed, neither water nor hay
    With Bill Brewer, Jan Stewer, Peter Gurney, Peter Davey, Dan'l Whiddon,
Harry Hawke, Bob Paul,
    Old Uncle Tom Cobley and all
    Old Uncle Tom Cobley and all.

3

They threw the owd halter right over her head
    All-along, down-along, out-along leigh
Tom Pearce's owd mare, her tumbled down dead
    With Bill Brewer, Jan Stewer, Peter Gurney, Peter Davey, Dan'l Whiddon,
Harry Hawke, Bob Paul,
    Old Uncle Tom Cobley and all
    Old Uncle Tom Cobley and all.

4

They sent for the parson and told him to hurry
    All-along, down-along, out-along leigh
Tom Pearce's owd mare her'lll have to be buried
    With Bill Brewer, Jan Stewer, Peter Gurney, Peter Davey, Dan'l Whiddon,
Harry Hawke, Bob Paul,
    Old Uncle Tom Cobley and all
    Old Uncle Tom Cobley and all.

5

They buried th'owd mare on the top of the hill
    All-along, down-along, out-along leigh
In the dead of the night you can hear his ghost still
    With Bill Brewer, Jan Stewer, Peter Gurney, Peter Davey, Dan'l Whiddon,
Harry Hawke, Bob Paul,
    Old Uncle Tom Cobley and all
    Old Uncle Tom Cobley and all.

VERSION 9
'Uncle Tam Cobley and All', 1867

George Philip Rigney Pulman collected this version at a 'Club Walk' of the Feniton Friendly Society in 1867. It has six verses and is twenty-two years earlier than Baring-Gould's version. Pulman noted 'One old gentleman, whose pipes he tells me are nearly worn out, gratifies me intensely by humming the following ditty'. His variant differs considerably from that published by Baring-Gould. At his death in 1880 it was claimed Pulman 'hated with an unquenchable hate the sham-nigger and music-hall style of what passes for music and humour and the people who gave entertainments of this class'.[210]

The second verse is similar to 'Widdicombe Fair' but the company of eleven riders has major differences: only Will Brewer, Jan Stewer and Tam Cobley are in both versions. There is no mention of Widecombe; the fair was replaced by 'Hoodycock' Fair. As mentioned earlier, similar lines had also been recorded in 1859:

Tom Pace, Tom Pace
Lend me your old mare
I wants en to ride up to Hoodicock Fair.

These lines were derived from J. F. Chanter who was born in Barnstaple in 1853 and later in his life, from 1886 onwards, was resident in the North Devon parish of Parracombe. Chanter. He claimed that 'an old man used to sing it at their servants' parties' in Barnstaple. In 1921 Chanter suggested that 'Hoodicot' had been used in versions older than 'Widdicombe Fair'.[211]

In 1888 T. C. Down of Plymouth recorded a similar word:

Tam Pearce he goes up 'pintap Oodycock Hill
An a sees his ole mare there a making hur will
    Way Will Brewer...[212]

In Devon hoodycock was a dialect word for a woodcock or poor soil.

Pulman was born at Axminster in 1819 and moved to Crewkerne where he acquired a printing and stationery business. His life work was as a journalist and publisher of several newspapers including *The Weekly News*. Music was a major interest and he had a long tenure as organist at the Minster Church in Axminster. Among his books was *The Song of Solomon in the East Devonshire Dialect* of which 250 copies were printed for Prince Louis Lucien Bonaparte whose hobby was the study of English dialect. Bonaparte had visited Exeter in 1859 and discussed Devon dialect with 'Nathan Hogg'. Pulman was aged 48 when he wrote the Feniton account and died eight years before the publication of 'Widdicombe Fair'.[213] His father (Philip) was born in Colyton, his mother (Ann) in London and his wife (Jane) in Axminster.

1

Tam Pearse, Tam Pearse, len me thine ole mare
    Al along, al along lane an a lee
That I mit ride down ta Hoodycock Vair
    Way Will Brewer, Jan Stewer, Clark Higgins,
    Giles Wiggins, Harry Oxley, Dick Hilsey,
    Will Welland, Tam Paul, Dick Chapman,
    Tom Backworthy, Ay Uncle Tam Cobley and all
        Ay Uncle Tam Cobley an all.

2

Now Tam Pearse's old mare hur wiz vayble an ole
    Al along, al along lane an a lee
An ha wanted tha old mare ta trat up tha mole
    Way Will Brewer, Jan Stewer, Clark Higgins,
    Giles Wiggins, Harry Oxley, Dick Hilsey,
    Will Welland, Tam Paul, Dick Chapman,
    Tom Backworthy, Ay Uncle Tam Cobley and all
        Ay Uncle Tam Cobley an all.

3

An when shill ez hev me ole mare back agean
    Al along, al along lane an a lee
Be Vridy nune ur a Zaturday zune
    Way Will Brewer, Clark Higgins,
    Giles Wiggins, Harry Oxley, Dick Hilsey,
    Will Welland, Tam Paul, Dick Chapman,
    Tom Backworthy, Ay Uncle Tam Cobley and all
        Ay Uncle Tam Cobley an all.

4

Now Vridy wiz pass'd, an Zaterday com
    All along, al along lane an a lee
Tam Pearse's old mare hur wadd'n com hom
    Way Will Brewer, Clark Higgins,
    Giles Wiggins, Harry Oxley, Dick Hilsey,
    Will Welland, Tam Paul, Dick Chapman,
    Tom Backworthy, Ay Uncle Tam Cobley and all
        Ay Uncle Tam Cobley an all.

5

Now Tam Pearse ha gose up pintap Hoodycock hill
    Al along, al along lane an a lee
Thare ha zees ez ole mare, hur wiz makin hur will
    Way Will Brewer, Clark Higgins,

Giles Wiggins, Harry Oxley, Dick Hilsey,
    Will Welland, Tam Paul, Dick Chapman,
Tom Backworthy, Ay Uncle Tam Cobley and all
    Ay Uncle Tam Cobley an all.

6

Now how dist thee naw thit et waz thine old mare
    Al along, al along, lane an a lee
Cuz wan vute wiz shude, an tother dree bare
    Way Will Brewer, Clark Higgins,
    Giles Wiggins, Harry Oxley, Dick Hilsey,
    Will Welland, Tam Paul, Dick Chapman,
    Tom Backworthy, Ay Uncle Tam Cobley and all
        Ay Uncle Tam Cobley an all.

VERSION 10
'Widdicombe Fair', 1916

This variant[214] of six verses was written by Charles Hubert Farnsworth, an American music academic,[215] and Cecil James Sharp, a leading figure in folk revival in England and a collaborator with Baring-Gould in *Songs of the West* and *English Folk Songs for Schools*. Sharp collected songs in Somerset and it was because of this that he concluded that 'Widdicombe Fair' was a copy of a Somerset song. Nevertheless, he retained Baring-Gould's title in this American collection of ballads.[216] Harry Hall is substituted for Harry Hawke.

1

Tam Pearce, Tam Pearce, lend me your grey mare
    All along, out along, down along lee
For I wants for to go to Widdicombe Fair
    Wi' Bill Brewer, Jan Stewer, Peter Gurney, Peter Davey, Dan'l Whidden,
Harry Hall, Old Uncle Tom Cobleigh and all
    Old Uncle Tom Cobleigh and all.

2

And when again shall I see my grey mare?
 All along, out along, down along lee
By Friday soon, or Saturday noon
 Wi' Bill Brewer, Jan Stewer, Peter Gurney, Peter Davey, Dan'l Whidden,
Harry Hall, Old Uncle Tom Cobleigh and all,
 Old Uncle Tom Cobleigh and all.

3

Well, Tam Pearce's old mare, her took sick and died
 All along, out along, down along lee
And when Tam heard the news, ur sat down and cried
 Wi' Bill Brewer, Jan Stewer, Peter Gurney, Peter Davey, Dan'l Whidden,
Harry Hall, Old Uncle Tom Cobleigh and all
 Old Uncle Tom Cobleigh and all.

4

But this isn't the end of this shocking affair
 All along, out along, down along lee
Nor, though they be dead, of the horrid career
 Of Bill Brewer, Jan Stewer, Peter Gurney, Peter Davey, Dan'l Whidden,
Harry Hall, Old Uncle Tom Cobleigh and all
 Old Uncle Tom Cobleigh and all.

5

When the wind whistles cold on the moor of a night
 All along, out along, down along lee
Tam Pearce's old mare doth appear gashly white!
Wi' Bill Brewer, Jan Stewer, Peter Gurney, Peter Davey, Dan'l Whidden,
Harry Hall, Old Uncle Tom Cobleigh and all
 Old Uncle Tom Cobleigh and all.

6

And all the night long be heard *skirling* and groans

    All along, out along, down along lee

From Tam Pearce's old mare, in her mouldering bones

    And from Bill Brewer, Jan Stewer, Peter Gurney, Peter Davey, Dan'l Whidden,

Harry Hall, Old Uncle Tom Cobleigh and all

    Old Uncle Tom Cobleigh and all

    Old Uncle Tom Cobleigh and all.

VERSION 11
'Widdecombe Fair', *c*.1884/1934

This variant, in nine verses, was collected by Charles James Maberly, a journalist, organist and singer in Berkshire, who noted it had been sung in 'Wessex' at least fifty years before. He sent it to *The Western Times* in 1934 and explained that the singers often changed the lines and that those 'who could introduce the most names of the company present was accounted the best songster'. Maberly also noted that 'the songster I have in mind prefaced his effort with two stentorian *hulloas*'. He also commented that Wessex men 'hated things coloured grey, hence probably the substitution of bay'. Maberly felt 'the melody sounded much older than that usually associated with the song.' He was born in Berkshire in 1867 but died in Exeter in 1935, the year after his letter was published. He does not appear to have had any Devon relations: neither parent was born in the West Country.[217]

1

Gaffer Pearce, Gaffer Pearce, lend we thy bay mare

    All along, down along, out along lea

Us do want for to go to Widdecombe Fair

    With Fowler and Marshall and Dixon and Wale,

    And Stumpy the Weaver the pot-bellied Gale,

    Old Uncle Tom Cobley and all.

2

And when do 'ee reckon to land home again?

    All along, down along, out along lea

A-Friday, for sure, by the light o' the moon

    With Fowler and Marshall and Dixon and Wale,

And Stumpy the Weaver the pot-bellied Gale,
    Old Uncle Tom Cobley and all.

3

But Friday comed and Saturday too
    All along, down along, out along lea
And yet ne'er a sign of the racketty crew
    With Fowler and Marshall and Dixon and Wale,
    And Stumpy the Weaver the pot-bellied Gale,
    Old Uncle Tom Cobley and all.

4

So Pearce, he crope up to the top of Bunthill
    All along, down along, out along lea
He were telled there'd a-been a terrible spill
    With Fowler and Marshall and Dixon and Wale,
    And Stumpy the Weaver the pot-bellied Gale,
    Old Uncle Tom Cobley and all.

5

He found 'em strewed all over the shop
    All along, down along, out along lea
The main on 'em dead, or ready to pop
    With Fowler and Marshall and Dixon and Wale,
    And Stumpy the Weaver the pot-bellied Gale,
    Old Uncle Tom Cobley and all.

6

The bonny bay mare were so hurted her died
    All along, down along, out along lea
And Pearce he flopped down on the bank and he cried,
(Spoken) Yes, bless ye. And didn't he just cuss
    Fowler and Marshall and Dixon and Wale,
    And Stumpy the Weaver the pot-bellied Gale,
(Sung) Old Uncle Tom Cobley and all.

7

And now when it comes round to Widdecombe night
    All along, down along, out along lea
The mare do show up in a cloud o' blue light
    With Fowler and Marshall and Dixon and Wale,
    And Stumpy the Weaver the pot-bellied Gale,
    Old Uncle Tom Cobley and all.

8

And the murk it be full of screetchin' and groans
    All along, down along, out along lea
And the clicketty click of rattley bones
    With Fowler and Marshall and Dixon and Wale,
    And Stumpy the Weaver the pot-bellied Gale,
    Old Uncle Tom Cobley and all.

9

And that be the tale of Widdecombe Fair
    All along, down along, out along lea
O the racketty crew and Pearce's bay mare
    With Fowler and Marshall and Dixon and Wale,
    And Stumpy the Weaver the pot-bellied Gale,
    Old Uncle Tom Cobley and all.

FAIR SONGS

VERSION 12
'Barnstaple Fair', 1899

This variant, in five verses, was collected by E. T. Wedmore,[218] who noted on the music sheet it had been 'sung by Rev. W. Chorley Loveband who has known it all 60 years. Vicar of West Down near Ilfracombe (for about 30 years), formerly of South Molton. Also sung by his father before him and his grandfather who was born at South Molton about 150 years ago'. It was presumably this version which had been sung twenty-one years earlier at South Molton with the title 'Sam Pearce's Mare'.[219]

    In 1899 William Chorley Loveband was 65 years old and he died in 1904.[220]

Edmund Tolson Wedmore was a Bristol sugar merchant who was 51 years old in 1899 and died in 1920. At his death it was noted that Wedmore 'was devoted to music and achieved considerable fame locally as an ardent musician… One of his most intimate friends was Mr Cecil J. Sharp'.[221] Wedmore also collected 'John Brown's Grey Mare' with Loveband on this day. It shares some similarities notably with the mare going down a hill and making her will.[222] In the lyrics to 'Barnstaple Fair' there is an explanation that 'daw' should be interpreted as dough.

1

Sam Pea'se, Sam Pea'se, len' me thy grey mare
 Ri-fol-a, rol-ri fol de
That I may ride to B'staple Fair wi' Jan Brewer, Harry Steer, Will Hawks,
Ned Whitton, Peter Davy, Will Garnsery,
 and the poor old Uncle Tom Cobley an' all.

2

Now Samuel Pea'se wive was so weak and so feeble
 Mavis, Pavis, Tiddy go round
 Mavis, Pavis, Tiddy go round
You know Her wanted th' ole Mare home to tread up the Daw!
 Way Jan Brewer, Harry Steer, Will Hawks, Ned Whitton, Peter Davy,
Will Garnsery,
 and the poor old Uncle Tom Cobley an' all.

3

Sam Pea'se went out upon the Hill
 Ri-fol-a, rol-ri fol de
 Ri-fol-a, rol-ri fol de
There 'e seed th' old Mare a making her will
 Wi' Jan Brewer, Harry Steer, Will Hawks, Ned Whitton, Peter Davy,
Will Garnsery,
 and the poor old Uncle Tom Cobley an' all.

4

How do you know that 'twas Samuel Pea'se's grey mare?

    Mavis, Pavis, Tiddy go round

    Mavis, Pavis, Tiddy go round

Her'd got wan a shu'd and th' t'other dree bare

    Wi' Jan Brewer, Harry Steer, Will Hawks, Ned Whitton, Peter Davy,

Will Garnsery,

    and the poor old Uncle Tom Cobley an' all.

5

Now Vriday was over, and Saturday was come

    Ri-fol-a, rol-ri fol de

    Ri-fol-a, rol-ri fol de

The poor ole mare wad'en come home

    Wi' Jan Brewer, Harry Steer, Will Hawks, Ned Whitton, Peter Davy,

Will Garnsery,

    and the poor old Uncle Tom Cobley an' all.

VERSION 13
'Midsummer Fair', 1904

This version in six verses, as sung by Joseph Cornelius in Somerset on 16 August 1904, was first collected by Cecil Sharp who wrote that:

'this is a variant of the Devonshire song "Widdecombe Fair"… I assume that some Widdecombe singer, probably in the latter half of last century, changed "Midsummer" into "Widdecombe" and substituted the names of local celebrities for the jingle of the last line. It is curious to note how these alterations at once gave new life to the ballad and popularised it, not only throughout Devonshire but pretty well all over England as well. I would claim for the Somerset air that it is older than the Devonshire tune and that it has more character and a better rhythm. Mr Marson added the last [sixth] verse, but in other respects the words are given here almost exactly as they were sung by Mr Cornelius.'

The well-known chorus, with its company, is absent and the fair at Widecombe has been replaced.[223] In other variants, sung in 1904 and 1907 at Castle Cary, the grey mare was ridden to Portsdown Fair with Uncle Tom Tobly. As with 'Widdicombe Fair' there was a company (Bill Brewer, Jack Steward, Harry Hawkins, John or Tom Trollop, Dick Joseph, Ben Bewlin or Bowlin, Ben Batway).[224] Later, in 1923, it was claimed that in about 1873 the Somerset version of 'Widdicombe Fair', as sung by men from the Mendips and the Moors, had the chorus:

Wi' Bill Brewer, Jan Stewer, Peter Davey, Peter Gurney, Sam Simkin,
Ben Beckaway, Dan'l Whidden, Harry Hawk and Tom Paul
　An' ol Uncle Tam Cobley an' all, an' all
　　Ol' Uncle Tam Cobley an' all.[225]

Bridgwater had a Midsummer Fair, as did Tiverton in Devon. Cornelius, and his family, were born in Shepton Beauchamp or Combe St Nicholas, all within easy reach of the Devon border.

This version has slightly different lyrics from those purportedly sung by Cornelius on the same date and in the same location. It was published in 1974:

2. When shall I have my grey mare back again?
　　Friday by noon or Saturday soon.
3. When Friday was gone and Saturday come
　　I saw the grey mare was not a-come home.
4. So When I came to the top of the hill
　　I saw the grey mare had been making her will.
5. So how did you know 'twas Tom Pearce's grey mare?
　　She had three new shoes and 't'other one bare.'[226]

1

Tom Pearce, Tom Pearce, lend me the grey mare
　　An-to-be-lone, a lallee-lal-lee
That I may go ride to some Midsummer Fair
　　To my oor, bag boor, bag nigger, bag waller, and ban-ta-ba-loo.

2

But can you return my grey nag again soon?
　An-to-be-lone, alallee-lal-lee
By Friday night or Saturday noon
　To my oor, bag boor, bag nigger, bag waller, and ban-ta-ba-loo.

3

But Friday was gone and Saturday come
　An-to-be-lone, alallee-lal-lee
And yet the grey mare was not a come home
　To my oor, bag boor, bag nigger, bag waller, and ban-ta-ba-loo.

4

So off I went to the top o' the hill
　An-to-be-lone, alallee-lal-lee
And saw the grey mare had been making her will
　To my oor, bag boor, bag nigger, bag waller, and ban-ta-ba-loo.

5

And how did you know it was Tommy's grey mare?
　An-to-be-lone, alallee-lal-lee
By three new shoes and t'other one bare
　To my oor, bag boor, bag nigger, bag waller, and ban-ta-ba-loo.

6

If ever I'm asked my horses to lend
　An-to-be-lone, alallee-lal-lee
I whisper this song in the ear of my friend
　To my oor, bag boor, bag nigger, bag waller, and ban-ta-ba-loo.

VERSION 14
'Portsdown Fair', 1907

This variant, in five verses, was collected by Cecil Sharp from a performance by John Gartell in Somerset in 1907. It was then claimed that Gartell had 'learned the song from an old shipmate in America forty years ago'.[227]

1

Tom Pearce, Tom Pearce, lend me your old mare
　　All along league along day
That I may ride to Portsdown Fair
　　With Bill Brewer, Jack Steward, Harry Hawkins, Tom Trollop, Dick Joseph,
Ben Bowlin, Ben Batway
　　　My Uncle Tom Tobly and all
　　　My Uncle Tom Tobly and all.

2

O when shall I see my old mare home again?
　　All along league along day
On Friday morn or Saturday soon
　　With Bill Brewer, Jack Steward, Harry Hawkins, Tom Trollop, Dick Joseph,
Ben Bowlin, Ben Batway
　　　My Uncle Tom Tobly and all
　　　My Uncle Tom Tobly and all.

3

Now Friday's gone and Saturday's come
　　All along league along day
And my old mare she has not returned home
　　With Bill Brewer, Jack Steward, Harry Hawkins, Tom Trollop, Dick Joseph,
Ben Bowlin, Ben Batway
　　　My Uncle Tom Tobly and all
　　　My Uncle Tom Tobly and all.

4

Tom Pearce he walked to Portsdown Fair
　　All along league along day
There he saw this old mare a-making her will
　　With Bill Brewer, Jack Steward, Harry Hawkins, Tom Trollop, Dick Joseph,
Ben Bowlin, Ben Batway
　　　My Uncle Tom Tobly and all
　　　My Uncle Tom Tobly and all.

5

Now he threw the halter all o'er the mare's head

All along league along day

Tom Pearce's old mare she fell down dead O

With Bill Brewer, Jack Steward, Harry Hawkins, Tom Trollop, Dick Joseph,

Ben Bowlin, Ben Batway

My Uncle Tom Tobly and all

My Uncle Tom Tobly and all.

VERSION 15
'Lansdown Fair', 1957–60

This variant, in five verses, was collected by Mervyn Plunkett between 1957 and 1960 as sung by George Maynard in West Sussex.[228] There were several other recordings by Maynard at this time. The lyrics in a version sung in 1959 are similar to those in this variant.[229] In 1953 a Sussex chorus was suggested as 'Bill Pitchfork, Jan Juglery, Peter Slybody, Peter Whiskey, Dan'l Devil, Harry Hollowbone, old Uncle Tom Hogsflesh and all'.[230]

1

Tom Pearce, Tom Pearce, lend me your old mare

Hey along, ding along, ding

Tom Pearce, Tom Pearce, lend me your old mare

Hey along, ding along, ding

For I want to ride over to Lansdown Fair with Bill Brewer, Jack Stewer, Arry

Orkins, Bill Josie, Arry Obbs, Tom Brown, Joe Chapman, Ben Backwell

And your Uncle Tom Cockrill and all

And your Uncle Tom Cockrill and all.

2

Oh when will my mare return home again?

Hey along, ding along, ding

Oh, at Friday noon, or Saturday soon

Hey along, ding along, ding

With Bill Brewer, Jack Stewer, Arry Orkins, Bill Josie, Arry Obbs, Tom Brown,

Joe Chapman, Ben Backwell

And your Uncle Tom Cockrill and all
And your Uncle Tom Cockrill and all.

3

Now Friday's gone and Saturday's come
Hey along, ding along, ding
And my old mare she's not return'd home
Hey along, ding along, ding
With Bill Brewer, Jack Stewer, Arry Orkins, Bill Josie, Arry Obbs, Tom Brown,
Joe Chapman, Ben Backwell
   And your Uncle Tom Cockrill and all
   And your Uncle Tom Cockrill and all.

4

Now I took a ride over to Lansdown Fair
   Hey along, ding along, ding
There I saw my old mare a-making her will
Hey along, ding along, ding
With Bill Brewer, Jack Stewer, Arry Orkins, Bill Josie, Arry Obbs, Tom Brown,
Joe Chapman, Ben Backwell
   And your Uncle Tom Cockrill and all
   And your Uncle Tom Cockrill and all.

5

He threw the halter right over her head
   Hey along, ding along, ding
And my old mare she dropp'd down dead
With Bill Brewer, Jack Stewer, Arry Orkins, Bill Josie, Arry Obbs, Tom Brown,
Joe Chapman, Ben Backwell
   And your Uncle Tom Cockrill and all boys
   And your Uncle Tom Cockrill and all.

VERSIONS 16a-b
Stow Fair, 1928 & 1916

These two versions were collected by H. Hurlbutt Albino at performances by Thomas Lanchbury in Gloucestershire[231] and Thomas Houndsome in Oxfordshire.[232] The titles, number of verses, names of the company and wording alter but they both substitute 'Uncle Tom Goblin' for Uncle Tom Cobley.

VERSION 16a
'Stow Fair', 1928

1

Tom Pearce, Tom Pearce, lend me your old mare
  Ho, ho, ho, hi, yo, Tom yo, Tom
Tom Pearce, Tom Pearce, lend me your old mare
With Bill Brewer, Jack Steward, Jerry Hawkins, Dick Joseph, Harry Hillop, Tom Bawling, Dick Chapman, Ben Paxwain, With your Uncle Tom Goblin and all
  With your Uncle Tom Goblin and all,

2

Tom Pearce old mare had gone to the fair
  Ho, ho, ho, hi, yo, Tom yo, Tom
Tom Pearce old mare had gone to the fair
  Ho, ho, ho, hi, yo, Tom yo, Tom
Tom Pearce old mare had gone to the fair
  Ho, ho, ho, hi, yo, Tom yo, Tom
With Bill Brewer, Jack Steward, Jerry Hawkins, Dick Joseph, Harry Hillop, Tom Bawling, Dick Chapman, Ben Paxwain, With your Uncle Tom Goblin and all,
  With your Uncle Tom Goblin and all,

3

When will Tom Pearce's old mare return?
  Ho, ho, ho, hi, yo, Tom yo, Tom
When will Tom Pearce's old mare return?
  Ho, ho, ho, hi, yo, Tom yo, Tom

When will Tom Pearce's old mare return?

    Ho, ho, ho, hi, yo, Tom yo, Tom

With Bill Brewer, Jack Steward, Jerry Hawkins, Dick Joseph, Harry Hillop, Tom Bawling, Dick Chapman, Ben Paxwain, With your Uncle Tom Goblin and all

    With your Uncle Tom Goblin and all,

4

Tom Pearce's old mare is tumbled down dead

    Ho, ho, ho, hi, yo, Tom yo, Tom

Tom Pearce's old mare is tumbled down dead

    Ho, ho, ho, hi, yo, Tom yo, Tom

Tom Pearce's old mare is tumbled down dead

    Ho, ho, ho, hi, yo, Tom yo, Tom

With Bill Brewer, Jack Steward, Jerry Hawkins, Dick Joseph, Harry Hillop, Tom Bawling, Dick Chapman, Ben Paxwain, With your Uncle Tom Goblin and all,

    With your Uncle Tom Goblin and all,

5

Tom Pearce's old mare is going to be buried

    Ho, ho, ho, hi, yo, Tom yo, Tom

Tom Pearce's old mare is tumbled down dead

    Ho, ho, ho, hi, yo, Tom yo, Tom

Tom Pearce's old mare is tumbled down dead

    Ho, ho, ho, hi, yo, Tom yo, Tom

With Bill Brewer, Jack Steward, Jerry Hawkins, Dick Joseph, Harry Hillop, Tom Bawling, Dick Chapman, Ben Paxwain, With your Uncle Tom Goblin and all

    With your Uncle Tom Goblin and all

VERSION 16b
'Tom Pierces' Old Mare', 1916

1

Tom Pierce, Tom Pierce, lend me your old mare
   Ho-o-o, Heigh-o
Tom Pierce, Tom Pierce, lend me your old mare
   Ho-o-o, Heigh-o
Tom Pierce, Tom Pierce, lend me your old mare
With Bill Brewer, Jack Steward, Jerry Hawkins, Dick Joseph, Freddy Hollocks,
Tom Bowles, Dick Chapman, Ben Backswain,
   And your Uncle Tom Goblin and all,
   Your Uncle Tom Goblin and all.

2

Tom Pierce's old mare is Tumbled Down dead
   Ho! Hey! Ho!
Tom Pierce's old mare is Tumbled Down dead
   Ho! Hey! Ho!
Tom Pierce's old mare is Tumbled Down dead
With Bill Brewer, Jack Steward, Jerry Hawkins, Dick Joseph, Freddy Hollocks,
Tom Bowles, Dick Chapman, Ben Backswain,
   And your Uncle Tom Goblin and all
   Your Uncle Tom Goblin and all.

3

Tom Pierce's old Mare is going to be buried
   Ho! Hey! Ho!
Tom Pierce's old Mare is going to be buried
   Ho! Hey! Ho!
Tom Pierce's old Mare is going to be buried
With Bill Brewer, Jack Steward, Jerry Hawkins, Dick Joseph, Freddy Hollocks,
Tom Bowles, Dick Chapman, Ben Backswain,
   And your Uncle Tom Goblin and all
   Your Uncle Tom Goblin and all.

VERSION 17
'Helston Fair', 1878

This variant was noted in 1934 as having been taken from a notebook kept by John Medley Doble in about 1878. The book's current location is unknown.[233] The three verses include notable differences from other versions, not only in respect of the identities of the excursionists but also in the fact that here they are depicted as travelling by cart.

1

Uncle Joe Maby lent me his old mare
    Ding-a-long, ding-a-long day
That we might go to Helston Fair
    Jim Stoor, Tom Blewer, Harry Holsey, Dick Tolsey, Tom Powell, Jim
Chapman, Bill Blackman
    And Uncle Joe Mayby and I.

2

Then up we got all into the cart
    Ding-a-long, ding-a-long day
And off we went with a steady trot
    Jim Stoor, Tom Blewer, Harry Holsey, Dick Tolsey, Tom Powell, Jim
Chapman, Bill Blackman
    And Uncle Joe Mayby and I.

3

Friday is gone, Saturday's come
    Ding-a-long, ding-a-long day
And they're not come home from Helston Fair
    Jim Stoor, Tom Blewer, Harry Holsey, Dick Tolsey, Tom Powell, Jim
Chapman, Bill Blackman
    And Uncle Joe Mayby and I.

VERSIONS 18a-b
Illsdown Fair, 1907

These two versions were collected by George Gardiner in Hampshire. The first was sung by Thomas Cooper in 1907[234] and the second by Thomas Hounsome by that year.[235] These differ between them in the wording and names of the company. Gardiner noted that they had 'practically the same form'.[236]

VERSION 18a
'Illsdown Fair', 1907

1

Joe Mabie, Joe Mabie, lend me your old mare
    All along, all along, ay
That we might ride over to Illsdown Fair
    Ding a long, ding along, day
With Bill Brewers, Jack Stewers, Harry Hawkins, Dick Josie, Harry Olive,
Tom Powell, Dick Chapman, Ben Blackman,
    And our Uncle Joe Mabie and all
    And our Uncle Joe Mabie and all.

2

When will you return again?
    All along, all along, ay
Oh Friday noon or Saturday soon
    Ding a long, ding along, day
With Bill Brewers, Jack Stewers, Harry Hawkins, Dick Josie, Harry Olive,
Tom Powell, Dick Chapman, Ben Blackman,
    And our Uncle Joe Mabie and all
    And our Uncle Joe Mabie and all.

3

Friday's gone and Saturday's come
    All along, all along, ay
Joe Mabie's mare is still standing there
    Ding a long, ding along, day

With Bill Brewers, Jack Stewers, Harry Hawkins, Dick Josie, Harry Olive,
Tom Powell, Dick Chapman, Ben Blackman,
  And our Uncle Joe Mabie and all
  And our Uncle Joe Mabie and all.

4

They throws the reins all over her head
  All along, all along, ay
When Joe Mabie's old mare she drops down dead there
  Ding a long, ding along, day
With Bill Brewers, Jack Stewers, Harry Hawkins, Dick Josie, Harry Olive,
Tom Powell, Dick Chapman, Ben Blackman,
  And our Uncle Joe Mabie and all
  And our Uncle Joe Mabie and all.

VERSION 18b
'Illsdown Fair', by 1907

1

Jo Maybie, Joe Maybie, lend me your old mare
  All along, all along, ay
Joy Maybie, Joe Maybie, lend me your old mare
  Ding along, ding along, day
That I might ride over to Illsdown Fair
With Bill Brewer, Jack Stewart, Harry Hawkins, Dick Chelsea, Harry Olive,
Tom Bowles, Dick Chapman, Ben Blackman,
  And your Uncle Joe Mabie and all
  Your Uncle Joe Mabie and all.

2

Oh when shall you return again
  All along, all along, ay
Oh when shall you return again
  Ding along, ding along, day
Friday at noon or Saturday soon

With Bill Brewer, Jack Stewart, Harry Hawkins, Dick Chelsea, Harry Olive,
Tom Bowles, Dick Chapman, Ben Blackman,
    And your Uncle Joe Mabie and all
    Your Uncle Joe Mabie and all.

3

Now Friday is gone and Saturday's come
    All along, all along, ay
Now Friday is gone and Saturday's come
    Ding along, ding along, day
Joe Mabie's old mare's not returned yet
With Bill Brewer, Jack Stewart, Harry Hawkins, Dick Chelsea, Harry Olive,
Tom Bowles, Dick Chapman, Ben Blackman,
    And your Uncle Joe Mabie and all
    Your Uncle Joe Mabie and all.

4

They threw the reins all over her neck
    All along, all along, ay
They threw the reins all over her neck
    Ding along, ding along, day
Joe Mabie's old mare fell dead at the fair
With Bill Brewer, Jack Stewart, Harry Hawkins, Dick Chelsea, Harry Olive,
Tom Bowles, Dick Chapman, Ben Blackman,
    And your Uncle Joe Mabie and all
    Your Uncle Joe Mabie and all.

VERSION 19
'Bedford Fair', 1960

This variant was collected by Fred Hamer from a performance by William Bartle in
1960. He explained 'in Bedfordshire this song was added to by the company, each singer
adding his contribution. I have here put together a number of typical contributions
into a consecutive story.'[237]

1

John Jones' old mare she's gone to the fair
    I, I, I, I, I, O
But most of 'em said she would never get there
    With Bill Brewitt, Jack Stewer, Tom Truman, Teddy Hawkins, Ben Bagway
    And your uncle Tom Cobber and I
    And your uncle Tom Cobber and I.

2

John Jones's old mare fell sick on the way
    I, I, I, I, I, O
And all she could do was to stand still and neigh
    With Bill Brewitt, Jack Stewer, Tom Truman, Teddy Hawkins, Ben Bagway
    And your uncle Tom Cobber and I
    And your uncle Tom Cobber and I.

3

John Jones he was sent for to fetch the old vet
    I, I, I, I, I, O
But he stopped on the way at a pub for a wet
    With Bill Brewitt, Jack Stewer, Tom Truman, Teddy Hawkins, Ben Bagway
    And your uncle Tom Cobber and I
    And your uncle Tom Cobber and I.

4

At last the vet came with his rusty old gun
    I, I, I, I, I, O
But the mare saw him coming and started to run
    With Bill Brewitt, Jack Stewer, Tom Truman, Teddy Hawkins, Ben Bagway
    And your uncle Tom Cobber and I
    And your uncle Tom Cobber and I.

5

John Jones' old mare she has tumbled down dead

   I, I, I, I, I, O

She died from her tail right up to her head

   With Bill Brewitt, Jack Stewer, Tom Truman, Teddy Hawkins, Ben Bagway

   And your uncle Tom Cobber and I

   And your uncle Tom Cobber and I.

CUMULATIVE FAIR SONGS

These songs share with 'Widdicombe Fair' choruses which elicited enthusiasm from the audience: each verse added names which rhymed with one another, such as Stewer and Brewer.

There are a number of other cumulative fair songs which complement those included in the following pages. The beggars in 'Craigbilly Fair', collected in 1925, comprised Rover and Kitty-lie-over, Rooney and Mooney, Nancy and Francey, Lily and Billy, Rabax and Old Madame Ball o' Wax, Dick and Old Lady Splooter Stick and Jamie and Joe.[238] The company in 'Donnybrook Fair', collected in 1929, comprised Ben and Old Mother Ben, Shake and Old Mother Shake-a-Leg, Nuts and Old Mother Funny Nuts, Sticks and Old Mother Fiddlesticks.[239] The beggars in 'Maligan Fair', collected in 1941, comprised Igo and Old Mother Bendigo, Stick and Old Mother Fiddlestick, Wax and Old Mother Ball o' Wax, Shake and Old Mother Shake-a-Leg, Drum and Old Mother Beat-a-Drum, Long and Old Mother Run-along, Cock and Old Mother Shuttlecock.[240]

VERSION 20
'The Beggars of Coldingham Fair', 1843

This version has three verses but in 1843 it was noted that there were additional ones. The editor wrote 'an immense number of odd names are strung together in loose rhymes. Young children appear as much delighted by these sounds as are youths and maidens with those smooth and musical couplets which fall so sweetly on a well-tuned ear, though any meaning may, as children say, be far to seek and ill to find.'[241]

1

The first time that I gaed to Coudingham Fair
I fell in with a jolly beggar
The beggar's name O it was Harry
And he had a wife and they called her Mary
    O Mary and Harry, and Harry and Mary
    And Janet and John
    That's the beggars one by one
    But now I will gi'e you them pair by pair
    All the brave beggars of Coudingham Fair.

2

The next time that I went to Coudingham Fair
There I met with another beggar
The beggar's name O it was Willie
And he had a wife and they called her Lillie
    And Harry and Mary, and Willie and Lillie
    And Janet and John
    That's the beggars one by one
    But now I will gi'e you them pair by pair
    All the brave beggars of Coudingham Fair.

3

The next time that I gaed to Coudingham Fair
I fell in with another beggar
The beggar's name O it was Wilkin
And he had a wife and they called her Gilkin
    And Harry and Mary, and Willie and Lillie
    And Wilkin and Gilkin, and Janet and John
    That's the beggars one by one
    Now I will gi'e you them pair by pair
    All the brave beggars of Coudingham Fair.

VERSION 21
'The Beggars of Ratcliffe Fair', 1849

This version, in ten verses, was printed in 1849.[242] Another published seventy years later also has ten verses but the names appear in a different order.[243]

1

As I went to Ratcliffe Fair, there I met with a jolly beggáre

Jolly beggáre and his name was John and his wife's name was Jumping Joan

    So there was John and Jumping Joan

    Merry companions every one.

2

As I went to Ratcliffe Fair, there I met with a jolly beggáre

Jolly beggáre and his name was Richard and his wife's name was Mrs Ap Richard

    So there was Richard and Mrs Ap Richard

    And there was John and Jumping Joan

    Merry companions every one.

3

As I went to Ratcliffe Fair, there I met with a jolly beggáre,

Jolly beggáre and his name was Robert and his wife's name was Mrs Ap Robert

    So was Robert and Mrs Ap Robert

    And there was Richard and Mrs Ap Richard

    And there was John and Jumping Joan

    Merry companions every one.

4

As I went to Ratcliffe Fair, there I met with a jolly beggáre,

Jolly beggáre and his name was Rice and his wife's name was Mrs Ap Rice

    So there was Rice and Mrs Ap Rice

    And there was Robert and Mrs Ap Robert

    And there was Richard and Mrs Ap Richard

    And there was John and Jumping Joan

    Merry companions every one.

5

As I went to Ratcliffe Fair, there I met with a jolly beggáre
Jolly beggáre and his name was Jones and his wife's name was Mrs Ap Jones
   So there was Jones and Mrs Ap Jones
   And there was Rice and Mrs Ap Rice
   And there was Robert and Mrs Ap Robert
   And there was Richard and Mrs Ap Richard
   And there was John and Jumping Joan
   Merry companions every one.

6

As I went to Ratcliffe Fair, there I met with a jolly beggáre,
Jolly beggáre and his name was Lloyd and his wife's name was Mrs Ap Lloyd
   So there was Lloyd and Mrs Ap Lloyd
   And there was Jones and Mrs Ap Jones
   And there was Rice and Mrs Ap Rice
   And there was Robert and Mrs Ap Robert
   And there was Richard and Mrs Ap Richard
   And there was John and Jumping Joan
   Merry companions every one.

7

As I went to Ratcliffe Fair, there I met with a jolly beggáre,
Jolly beggáre and his name was Owen and his wife's name was Mrs Ap Owen
   So there was Owen and Mrs Ap Lewin
   And there was Lloyd and Mrs Ap Lloyd
   And there was Jones and Mrs Ap Jones
   And there was Rice and Mrs Ap Rice
   And there was Robert and Mrs Ap Robert
   And there was Richard and Mrs Ap Richard
   And there was John and Jumping Joan
   Merry companions every one.

8

As I went to Ratcliffe Fair, there I met with a jolly beggáre,
Jolly beggáre and his name was Lewin and his wife's name was Mrs Ap Lewin
    So there was Lewin and Mrs Ap Lewin
    And there was Owen and Mrs Ap Lewin
    And there was Lloyd and Mrs Ap Lloyd
    And there was Jones and Mrs Ap Jones
    And there was Rice and Mrs Ap Rice
    And there was Robert and Mrs Ap Robert
    And there was Richard and Mrs Ap Richard
    And there was John and Jumping Joan
    Merry companions every one

9

As I went to Ratcliffe Fair, there I met with a jolly beggáre,
Jolly beggáre and his name was Shenkyn and his wife's name was Mrs Ap
Shenkyn
    So there was Shenkyn and Mrs Ap Shenkyn
    And there was Lewin and Mrs Ap Lewin
    And there was Owen and Mrs Ap Lewin
    And there was Lloyd and Mrs Ap Lloyd
    And there was Jones and Mrs Ap Jones
    And there was Rice and Mrs Ap Rice
    And there was Robert and Mrs Ap Robert
    And there was Richard and Mrs Ap Richard
    And there was John and Jumping Joan
    Merry companions every one.

10

As I went to Ratcliffe Fair, there I met with a jolly beggáre,
Jolly beggáre and his name was Howell and his wife's name was Mrs Ap Howell
    So there was Howell and Mrs Ap Howell
    And there was Shenkyn and Mrs Ap Shenkyn
    And there was Lewin and Mrs Ap Lewin
    And there was Owen and Mrs Ap Lewin

And there was Lloyd and Mrs Ap Lloyd

And there was Jones and Mrs Ap Jones

And there was Rice and Mrs Ap Rice

And there was Robert and Mrs Ap Robert

And there was Richard and Mrs Ap Richard

And there was John and Jumping Joan

Merry companions every one.

VERSION 22

'Jolly Companions' or 'Widlicombe Fair', 1953

This song has eight verses and was sung in Norfolk by Harry Cox in 1953.[244] It appears to be only loosely connected with 'Widdicombe Fair'.

1

As I was a-going to Wid-li-combe Fair

Jolly old baker I met there

This old baker, his name it was Balls

His old woman was Old Mother Bags o' Balls

    So there was Balls, Old Mother Bags o' Balls,

    Johnny and Jumping Joan –

    Jolly companions everyone.

2

As I was a-going to Wid-li-combe Fair

Jolly old cobbler I met there

This old cobber, his name it was Wax

His old woman was Old Mother Balls o' Wax

    Then there was Wax, Old Mother Balls o' Wax,

    Balls, Old Mother Bags o' Balls,

    Johnny and Jumping Joan –

    Jolly companions everyone.

3

As I was a-going to Wid-li-combe Fair
Jolly old fiddler, his name it was Dicks
His old woman was Old Mother Fiddle-sticks
    Then there was Dicks, Old Mother Fiddle-sticks,
    Wax, Old Mother Balls o' Wax,
    Balls, Old Mother Bags o' Balls,
    Johnny and Jumping Joan,
    Jolly companions everyone.

4

As I was a-going to Wid-li-combe Fair
Jolly old tailor, his name it was Pins
His old woman was Old Mother Prickle-pins
    Then there was Pins, Old Mother Pricklepins,
    Dicks, Old Mother Fiddle-sticks,
    Wax, Old Mother Balls o' Wax,
    Balls, Old Mother Bags o' Balls,
    Johnny and Jumping Joan,
    Jolly companions everyone.

5

As I was a-going to Wid-li-combe Fair
Jolly old weaver, his name it was Darns
His old woman was Old Mother Balls o' Yarn
    Then there was Yarn, Old Mother Balls of Yarn,
    Pins, Old Mother Pricklepins,
    Dicks, Old Mother Fiddle-sticks,
    Wax, Old Mother Balls o' Wax,
    Balls, Old Mother Bags o' Balls,
    Johnny and Jumping Joan,
    Jolly companions everyone.

6

As I was a-going to Wid-li-combe Fair
Jolly old Miller, his name was Shake
His old woman was Old Mother Shake-a-leg
    Then there was Shake, Old Mother Shake-a-leg,
    Yarn, Old Mother Balls of Yarn,
    Pins, Old Mother Pricklepins,
    Dicks, Old Mother Fiddle-sticks,
    Wax, Old Mother Balls o' Wax,
    Balls, Old Mother Bags o' Balls,
    Johnny and Jumping Joan,
    Jolly companions everyone.

7

As I was a-going to Wid-li-combe Fair
Jolly old tinker his name it was Pots
His old woman was Old Mother Slobberchops
    Then there was Pots, Old Mother Slobberchops,
    Shake, Old Mother Shake-a-leg,
    Yarn, Old Mother Balls of Yarn,
    Pins, Old Mother Pricklepins,
    Dicks, Old Mother Fiddle-sticks,
    Wax, Old Mother Balls o' Wax,
    Balls, Old Mother Bags o' Balls,
    Johnny and Jumping Joan,
    Jolly companions everyone.

8

As I was a-going to Wid-li-combe Fair
Some bloody idiot I met there
This bloody idiot, his name was Nuts
His old woman was Old Mother Funny-nuts
    Then were was Nuts, Old Mother Funny-nuts,
    Pots, Old Mother Slobberchops,
    Shake, Old Mother Shake-a-leg,

Yarn, Old Mother Balls of Yarn,
Pins, Old Mother Pricklepins,
Dicks, Old Mother Fiddle-sticks,
Wax, Old Mother Balls o' Wax,
Balls, Old Mother Bags o' Balls,
Johnny and Jumping Joan,
Jolly companions everyone.

FIRST WORLD WAR

'Widdicombe Fair' remained a popular song throughout the war both in Britain, particularly in England and also overseas. Three versions were written about the war.

VERSION 23
'English *Volkslied*', 1914

This *volkslied*, or folk song, appeared four months after the start of the Great War. In 1914 these lyrics appeared in one English national newspaper report with a preceding note that 'according to a German map of England, only Devonshire and Cornwall will remain British territory at the end of the war'. This parody includes the names of not only the narrator (*meinself*) who was, presumably, the German Emperor William II, but also that of God and the German Chancellor (Theobald Theodor Friedrich Alfred von Bethman-Hollweg), Chief of Staff (Helmuth von Moltke the Younger) as well as the Crown Prince (Wilhelm) and three of the Prussian princes (Joachim, Adalbert and Eitel Friedrich). It also includes Franz Joseph, Emperor of Austria.[245] The tune was noted as being that of 'Widdicombe Fair'.

1

Jan Bull, Jan Bull, give me thy grey coast
All along Channel and up the North Sea
For I'm planning to gobble your island on toast
Yorkshire Pudding, Norfolk Dumpling, Welsh Rarebit, Southdown Mutton.
Dorset Butter, Kent Hops
　　The Roast Beef of Old England and all!
　　The Roast Beef of Old England and all!

2

And what will be spared to Jan Bull of your greed?

Cornwall and Devonshire's zidy and cream

I cannot spare more, I've too many to feed

There's Joachim, and Adalbert, Eitel Friedrich, Bethmann-Hollweg, Von Moltke, Francis Joseph,

The Kronprinz, Meinself, Gott *und* all

The Kronprinz, Meinself, Gott *und* all!

VERSION 24
'Old Uncle Tom Cobley at War', 1915

This version was written by Wallace Masland of Tiverton and published in 1915. He was born in 1870 in Somerset and worked as an auctioneer's bookkeeper. The ballad was performed during the war at Hennock, Colchester and in London[246] and a recording was made by Charles Tree, an Exeter baritone.[247] It was probably this ballad which met with approval in Buckingham in 1916. It was said to have been 'a much appreciated parody on Widdicombe Fair in which Tom Price [sic] and his old mare go to Germany'.[248]

The purpose of this version appears to have been to encourage men to enlist for the services before conscription was introduced in 1916. Two key military figures are mentioned: Herbert Kitchener was Secretary of State for War and Alexander von Kluck was in command of the German First Army.

1

Tom Pearce, Tom Pearce, lend me thy grey mare

To go all-along, out-along Germany way

For I wants to give thick old Kaiser a scare

With Bill Brewer, Jan Stewer, Peter Gurney, Peter Davey, Danl Whiddon, 'Arry Hawke, Old Uncle Tom Cobley, and all.

2

Well, Tom Pearce's old mare and me goes out to war

All-along, out-along Germany way

And I'd very soon killed 50 Germans or more

With Bill Brewer, Jan Stewer, Peter Gurney, Peter Davey, Danl. Whiddon, 'Arry Hawke, Old Uncle Tom Cobley, and all.

The Kaiser, *c*1910–1915.

3

Our doings gets round to headquarters, I think
    All-along, out-along Germany way
For Lord Kitchener says: I be standing a drink
    For Bill Brewer, Jan Stewer, Peter Gurney, Peter Davey, Danl. Whiddon, 'Arry Hawke, Old Uncle Tom Cobley, and all.

4

Thick old mare lay one night in the trenches with me
    All-along, out-along Germany way
Twas so quiet I was boiling the kittle for tea
    For Bill Brewer, Jan Stewer, Peter Gurney, Peter Davey, Danl. Whiddon, 'Arry Hawke, Old Uncle Tom Cobley, and all.

5

All to onst there was firing and shouting and sich
    All-along, out-along Germany way
And 200 Germans jumps into our ditch
    On Bill Brewer, Jan Stewer, Peter Gurney, Peter Davey, Danl. Whiddon, 'Arry Hawke, Old Uncle Tom Cobley, and all.

6

Thick old mare was disturbed with the terrible row
    All-along, out-along Germany way
And her jumps up and hollies like any old cow
    So did Bill Brewer, Jan Stewer, Peter Gurney, Peter Davey, Danl. Whiddon, 'Arry Hawke, Old Uncle Tom Cobley, and all.

7

Kaiser Bill sees the mare, and he turns gashly white
    All-along, out-along Germany way
And he ses to old Kluck, all a-trembling with fright
    There's Von Brewer, Von Stewer, Von Gurney, Von Davey, Von Whiddon, Von Hawke, Old Uncle Von Cobley and all.

8

Well, us chased thick old Kaiser through hedges and stiles   All-along, out-along
Germany way
I suppose that I rin pretty near 40 miles
    With Bill Brewer, Jan Stewer, Peter Gurney, Peter Davey, Danl. Whiddon,
'Arry Hawke, Old Uncle Tom Cobley, and all.

9

Then the Kaiser he gives us the slip in a fog
    All-along, out-along Germany way
And me and the mare us gets stugged in a bog
    With Bill Brewer, Jan Stewer, Peter Gurney, Peter Davey, Danl. Whiddon,
'Arry Hawke, Old Uncle Tom Cobley, and all.

10

Tom Pearce's old mare then her took sick and died
    All along, out-along Germany way
And I don't mind admitting I sot down and cried
    With Bill Brewer, Jan Stewer, Peter Gurney, Peter Davey, Danl. Whiddon,
'Arry Hawke, Old Uncle Tom Cobley, and all.

11

I could tell 'ee lots more of the glories of war
    All-along, out-along Germany way
But I wants tu get back just to kill a few more
    With Bill Brewer, Jan Stewer, Peter Gurney, Peter Davey, Danl. Whiddon,
'Arry Hawke, Old Uncle Tom Cobley, and all.

12

Now, when the war's over, I know you'll be vexed
    You young chaps what stays home on some cowardly pretext
For you'll find all the gals with their arms round t' necks
    Of Bill Brewer, Jan Stewer, Peter Gurney, Peter Davey, Danl. Whiddon,
Arry Hawke, Old Uncle Tom Cobley, and all.

VERSION 25
'War Song of Number Two Section', 1915

This variant appeared in a servicemen's magazine in 1915. The writer was anonymous. The verses concern the night watch of HMS *Defence* and the seven named men include Francis Melville Prattent, Acting Lieutenant RNR, who died ten months later, along with all of the ship's crew of 904 men, during the Battle of Jutland in May and June 1916.[249] Presumably all six of the other crewmembers had transferred from HMS *Defence* before the battle.

The final verse was added because 'The singing or so-called singing of this song invariably raised such loud applause that the brains of Number Two section were long ago brought to bear on the construction of an 'Encore' verse.' The verses were preceded by explanatory text:

> The inclusion of Bill Bailey's name into the chorus may evoke some discussion, but on the famous night when this song was composed, it was found that there were not enough Officers in Number Two section to supply the names to completely fill the chorus, so it was decided to include the voice pipe man.

A discussion then arose as to the name of this voice pipe man and in the opinion of one officer (expressed very forcibly) the name was Bailey. It was not until the song had been sung on several occasions that it was discovered that Bailey belonged to another section. However, the name fitted well into the chorus so it was allowed to stand; although it has been rumoured that intense jealousy has been caused among the voice pipe operators and that Voice Pipe Bill Baily has on several occasions had to defend with his fists the great honour done to him in including his name in the chorus of so notable a song.'

1

Now we have a good ship, and her name's the *Defence*
    All along, down along, over the sea
And each evening we go to Night Defence
    With O. Bevir, Frank Prattent, Garge Proctor, Dick Everett, Garge Moore,
Bill Bailey, Old Uncle John Champion and all
    Old Uncle John Champion and all.

2

Just see all the officers run helter skelter
  All along, down along, over the sea
And the ones that are going to Number Two shelter
  Are O. Bevir, Frank Prattent, Garge Proctor, Dick Everett, Garge Moore,
Bill Bailey, Old Uncle John Champion and all
  Old Uncle John Champion and all.

3

The guns are given a range and deflection
  All along, down along, over the sea
And all is correct with Number Two Section
  And O. Bevir, Frank Prattent, Garge Proctor, Dick Everett, Garge Moore,
Bill Bailey, Old Uncle John Champion and all
  Old Uncle John Champion and all.

4

Then according to somebody's pre-arranged plan
  All along, down along, over the sea
Our section is told the fore guns to man
  With O. Bevir, Frank Prattent, Garge Proctor, Dick Everett, Garge Moore,
Bill Bailey, Old Uncle John Champion and all
  Old Uncle John Champion and all.

5

Next, in order to train the man at the voice pipe
  All along, down along, over the sea
They pass down some absolute terrible tripe
  From O. Bevir, Frank Prattent, Garge Proctor, Dick Everett, Garge Moore,
Bill Bailey, Old Uncle John Champion and all
  Old Uncle John Champion and all.

6

Now some sleep with a blanket, and some with a rug
    All along, down along, over the sea
But all of us like a jolly good fug
    With O. Bevir, Frank Prattent, Garge Proctor, Dick Everett, Garge Moore,
Bill Bailey, Old Uncle John Champion and all
    Old Uncle John Champion and all.

7

When the dawn is breaking and the clock strikes four
    All along, down along, over the sea
The bugler wakes up and sounds the 'Secure'
    For O. Bevir, Frank Prattent, Garge Proctor, Dick Everett, Garge Moore,
Bill Bailey, Old Uncle John Champion and all
    Old Uncle John Champion and all.

Encore verse

Now its no good you're getting a fit of the blues
    All along, down along, over the sea
For when the fight comes we can't possibly lose
    With O. Bevir, Frank Prattent, Garge Proctor, Dick Everett, Garge Moore,
Bill Bailey, Old Uncle John Champion and all
    Old Uncle John Champion and all.

SECOND WORLD WAR

These two versions relate to journalism during the Second World War. The first expounds on the effect that the war restricted the number of nonsensical stories on oversized fruit, the Loch Ness Monster or on 'beach girls'. One such story of 1936 concerned a 96 year old man from Garston who returned from the Isle of Man and commented 'I am disgusted with the half-naked girls I have seen. Lip-stick, make-up and as little clothing as possible seems to be their only desire'.[250] The second variant was written about the BBC's newsreaders.

VERSION 26
Untitled (Loch Ness Monster), 1940

This variant was untitled and written by 'Ratz'. It has four verses and was printed in January, 1940.[251] The piece was headed 'A Northern paper asks for news of the Loch Ness Monster'.

1

Loch Ness, Loch Ness (said I to my Muse)
    Up along, all along, down along lee
Your mythical Monster was rated as news
    In the gay days of peace-time, how distant they be
With the Heat Wave, the Cold Snap, the Beach Girl, the Crisis, the Great Giant Gooseberry and all.

2

The weather is banished from headline and mike
    Up along, down along, all along lee
Now nobody knows what the climate is like
    And we're ignorant what kind of weather it be
If it's freezing, sun-shining, cloud-bursting, fair, settled or a proper pea-souper and all.

3

The Beach Girl had vanished – we see her no more
    Up along, down along, down all lee
A-bouncing of medicine balls on the shore
    We're inclined to suspect that a sergeant is she
In the Women's Auxiliary Territorial Service
    it's the deuce of a mouthful and all.

4

The Crisis has vanished – it's now done its stuff
    Up along, down along, like the *Graf Spee*
And as for the Monster – there's monsters enough
    As I'm certain, dear reader, you'll promptly agree

With Joe Stalin, Hermann Goering, Joe Goebbels, Heinrich Himmler, Joachim Ribbentrop and old Uncle Adolf and all.

VERSION 27

'And this is – reading it', 1941

This parody was written in three verses by Michael Barsley in 1941 and noted as having the 'tune of Widdecombe Fair'. The individuals named were then all well-known as newsreaders.[252]

1

Tom Pierce, Tom Pierce, not a moment to lose!
    Eight o'clock, one o'clock, B.B.C.
Come turn on the wireless and let's hear the news
    From Bruce Belfrage, Alan Howland, Frederick Allen, Joe Macleod,
    Frank Phillips and Alvar Liddell,
    Frank Phillips and Alvar Liddell!

2

Tom Pierce, Tom Pierce, 'tis the voice of Big Ben
    Six o'clock, nine o'clock, B.B.C.
And now for the voice of those versatile men
    Bruce Belfrage, Alan Howland, Frederick Allen, Joe Macleod,
    Frank Phillips and Alvar Liddell,
    Frank Phillips and Alvar Liddell

3

On the day they announce that our victory 's won
    Seven to twelve o'clock, B.B.C.
I suggest an impressive male chorus be done
    By Bruce Belfrage, Alan Howland, Frederick Allen, Joe Macleod,
    Frank Phillips and Alvar Liddell,
    Frank Phillips and Alvar Liddel

The BBC parody of 1941.

ADVERTISING

Advertisers wrote parodies to sell products such as Ramsden's Riding, an ale made in Halifax. In 1952 the company ran an ad:

> Tom Pearce, Tom Pearce lend my thy grey mare
> > All along, down along, out along lea!
> An let me away now to Halifax Fair
> > Wi' Bill Brewer, Jan Stewer, Peter Davey, Dan Widden, 'Arry 'Awke,
> > For a bottle of *Riding* an' all!
> > A bottle of *Riding* an' all![253]

In 1945 the ballad was parodied to advertise performances at a Scottish theatre.

Three One-Act Plays

> St James's Hall and get up them stairs
> > All along, down along, out along lee
> For I want to see the Forfar New Players
> > With Fred Milne, Connie Tair, Jean Lowson, Jean Smith, Hilda Stewart,
> Helen Lamond,
> > And Auntie Macquarie and all
> > And Auntie Macquarie and all
>
> But when do you want those players to see?
> > All along, down along, out along lee
> Oh! Thursday, Friday, Sat'day suits me
> > With Nan Troup, Phyllis Guild, Norah Macfarlane, Nora Ell, May Collie,
> Anna Hill,
> > And Auntie Macquarie and all
> > And Auntie Macquarie and all.[254]

VERSION 28
'Barnstaple Fair', 1934

The song was adapted for the *North Devon Journal* to promote Barnstaple Fair in 1934.[255]

1

As I was going to Barnstaple Fair
　Up along, out along, down along Lee
In Joy Street I heard a man singing this air
　With Ted Thomas, Charlie Phillips, Georgie Hill, Bertie Searle, Elsie Taylor,
Pyke Jarvis, Jimmy Ridge, Stan Lile, Jack Bond
　　Old Uncle Bill Thomas and all
　　Old Uncle Bill Thomas and all!!

2

Now listen you folk, with money to spare
　Up along, out along, down along Lee
Just wander down Joy Street, and squander it there
　With George Gale, Billy Hoare, Ray Furse, George Marshall, Sam Ayre, Bill
Richards, Frank Edwards, Stan Bowden, Barum Bakers
　　Old Uncle Frank Dyson and all
　　Old Uncle Frank Dyson and all!!

3

Oh! Joy Street is right in the midst of the Town
　Up along, down along, out along Lee
It's easy to find, and you won't be let down by
　Billy Hoare, George Gale, Ray Furse, Frank Dyson, Sam Ayre, Bill Richards,
Frank Edwards, Stan Bawden, Barum Bakers
　　Old Uncle George Marshall and all,
　　Old Uncle George Marshall and all!!

4

The moral of this song is plain to behold
　Up along, down along, out along Lee
For Joy Street is well stocked with goods to be sold by
　Bill Thomas, Charlie Phillips, Georgie Hill, Bertie Searle, Pyke Jarvis, Elsie
Taylor, Jim Ridge, Stand Lile, Jack Bond
　　Old Uncle Ted Thomas and all
　　Old Uncle Ted Thomas and all!!

VERSION 29
Untitled (Plymouth Whisky), 1909

In June 1909 the ballad was used by Picken & Company, wine and spirit merchants in Whimple Street in Plymouth, to advertise 'Western Blend' Scotch Whisky, 'the whiskey with a Westcountry name and a world-wide reputation for age and excellence'. That year readers of *The Western Morning News* learned that the whisky was 'as well known as Bill Brewer, Jan Stewer, Peter Gurney, Peter Davey, Dan'l Widdon, Harry Hawk, Old Uncle Tom Cobley and all.' The advertisement subsequently included a variation of 'Widdicombe Fair'.[256] The first of five verses placed the Company on Huccaby Tor, just above Dartmeet on Dartmoor.

1

Down tew Plymouth the volks do be askin' whaffer
    All along, down along, out along, lee
There was gathered last week upon Huccaby Tor
    Bill Brewer, Jan Stewer, Peter Gurney,
    Peter Davy, Dan'l Whiddon, Harry Hawk,
    Old Uncle Tom Cobbly, and all.

2

Ver seeing as 'ow the ole mare be dead
    All along, down along, out along, lee
Us vancies there wusn't no more tew be said
    'Bout Bill Brewer, Jan Stewer, Peter Gurney,
    Peter Davy, Dan'l Whiddon, Harry Hawk,
    Old Uncle Tom Cobbly, and all.

3

But it zims that the Dock had heered tell o' that band
    All along, down along, out along, lee
And said as 'e wanted tew shake by the hand
    Bill Brewer, Jan Stewer, Peter Gurney,
    Peter Davy, Dan'l Whiddon, Harry Hawk,
    Old Uncle Tom Cobbly, and all.

4

And now when they gather his health vor to drink
    All along, down along, out along, lee
By Garge, we must have the best liquor, I think
    Says Bill Brewer, Jan Stewer, Peter Gurney,
    Peter Davy, Dan'l Whiddon, Harry Hawk,
    Old Uncle Tom Cobbly, and all.

5

Down tew Plymouth the volks be sayin' the same
    All along, down along, out along, lee
O' the Whisky that goes by a Westcountry Name
    Says Bill Brewer, Jan Stewer, Peter Gurney,
    Peter Davy, Dan'l Whiddon, Harry Hawk,
    Old Uncle Tom Cobbly, and all.

VERSION 30
'Penny Wise or Did–he-come-Fair', 1932

In the summer of 1932 Shell Oil Corporation adapted 'Widdicombe Fair' with the message 'You are SAFE with SHELL OIL'. It followed a campaign entitled 'Sad Story of Jack's Cheap-Jack Oil'. The year before, in 1931, the company had adapted, in a similar manner, 'I remember!' by Thomas Hood.[257]

1

OH boy can you sell me some oil very cheap
    All along, down along, out along lee?
O sell me the cheapest old oil that you keep
    For my engine, my gear box, my chassis, my big-ends
    My bearings, my pistons, my little valve tappets and all,
      My little valve tappets and all.

2

OH no Sir, I only sell oil with a name
    All along, down along, out along tee
To use a cheap oil in your car is a shame

On your engine, your gear box, your chassis, your big-ends
Your bearings, your pistons, your little valve tappets and all
Your little valve tappets and all.

3

BUT the owner insisted and went for his ride
 All along, down along, out along tee
With a quart of the cheapest (and nameless) inside
 For his engine, his gear box, his chassis, his big-ends
 His bearings, his pistons, his little valve tappets and all
 His little valve tappets and all,

4

HE hadn't gone long and he hadn't gone far
 All along, down along, out along lee
When he heard a most horrible noise in his car
 From his engine, his gear box, his chassis, his big-ends
 His bearings, his pistons, his little valve tappets and all
 His little valve tappets and all.

5

AND this was the end of this horrid affair
 All along, down along, out along lee
He paid a big bill for the cost of repair
 To his engine, his gear box, his chassis, his big-ends
 His bearings, his pistons, his little valve tappets and all
  His little valve tappets and all.

6

THE Garage boy told him, and I say as well
 All along, down along, out along lee
Cheap oil is expensive – the wise 'uns use Shell
 For their engine, their gearbox, their chassis, their big-ends
 Their bearings, their pistons, their little valve tappets
  Their little valve tappets and all.

VERSION 31
'Mare and Corporation', 1947

This operatic version promoted Guinness in 1947. The advertiser invented the most novel story line in any parody of 'Widdicombe Fair'.[258]

1

Tom Pearce, Tom Pearce, will you tell us what course
    (All along, out along, down along lea)
You took to develop the thews of a horse
    Like Carnera, Goliath, Eugene Sandow, Gog and Magog, Paul Bunyan,
Asar Thor,
    And Popeye the Sailor and all, and Popeye the Sailor and all.

2

My mare, you remember, so lately deceased
    (By the terms of her will I'm the sole legatee)
Was in several respects a remarkable beast
    Like Bucephalus, Prince Regent, Hrimfaxi, Copenhagen, Black Beauty,
Brown Bess,
    (Eohippus was rather too small, Eohippus was rather too small.)

3

Although, being horse, she could not herself sing
    A prop of the opera nightly was she
For she carried the diva through most of The Ring
    And Tannhäuser, Don Juan, Leonora, Traviata, Trovatore, Pagliacci,
    And old Uncle Siegfried and all, and old Uncle Siegfried and all.

4

She died; and to carry the vast prima-donna
    (Seventeen stone) now devolved upon me
Bring Guinness! I cried, *or Tom Pearce is a gonner!*
Not zibbib, nor arrak, nor toddy, nor metheglin, nor date-beer, nor tedj
    Bring Guinness or nothing at all! Bring Guinness or nothing at all.

5

The dame was amazed by her spirited mount
    And ever since then I'm a strong devotee
Of Guinness, whose virtues are quite without count
    And for goodness, and richness, body-building,
    Frame-filling, muscle-making, good health,
    A Guinness is good for us all, a Guinness is good for us all.

LOCAL AND NATIONAL POLITICS

Nine political parodies have been identified. These refer to both national and local politics. Two were written to support Liberal and Conservative parliamentary candidates. Three relate to Devon: these concern Dartmouth in 1869, Tavistock in 1910 and Barnstaple in 1910. There is also a version in Devon dialect about the Pension Act of 1907. Two others are concerned with local politics in the London communities of Golders Green and Willesden.

VERSION 32
'An excellent new ballad to the tune of Old Cobley, &c', 1761

This ballad was printed in response to Exeter's Parliamentary election of 1761 and may, possibly, be related to 'Widdicombe Fair'; it appeared as a broadside, the single song sheets that were sold cheaply in the streets. Individuals mentioned include the Whig candidate William Mackworth Praed (Mac Billy), an Exeter merchant, and Sir Richard Warwick Bampfylde of Poltimore (Lord Petulant Flat), former MP of Exeter. Praed, who was supported by the Dissenters and stood in opposition to the city council, had lost the election and the ballad lampoons his election to the mock seat of Ide. The reference to the 'tune of Old Cobley' could have been to Tom Cobley but there was another citing of him a few years earlier: verses regarding the Ide election in 1754 included 'the election for Ide is over we hear, Old Cobley declined it and would not appear'.[259]

An Excellent New
BALLAD.

To the Tune of Old Cobley, &c.

THE Election for *Exeter*'s over we find,
    Mac Billy was flung, and came *first in behind*,
He brandish'd his Lath, he cry'd, and he swore,
To see *Seven* Hundred Votes dwindled to *Four*.

On *Monday* the Thirtieth of *March* last at *Noon*,
The *Dyer*, Old *Cruxy*, and *A——w B——n*,
Sat out in *Post-Wheelbarrows* all, 'tis agreed,
To set up *Mac Billy* a Member for *Ide*.

But the Sons of Mount *Ida* their Rights to maintain,
Rejected their Offer and Bribes with Disdain,
And bid them not act like such infamous Tools,
For the Freemen of *Ide* hated *B——ns* and *Fools*.

Huzzaing for *Billy*, and waving his Hat,
The next that advanc'd was *Lord Petulant Flat*,
Who swore the Election should not be delay'd,
For he was a *Lord*, and he would be obey'd.

The honest Electors then boldly reply'd,
We all are *Cobleans*, and scorn to change Side;
Then for *Morrish* and *Odam* aloud they did bawl,
For *Morrish* and *Odam*, Huzza! one and all.

To chuse me, says *Mac*, if you do not think fit,
I'll ride up to *London*, and get a *New Writ*.
A Writ, replies *Morrish*, with a comical Grin,
For yourself, I presume, at the Suit of Old *Phin!*

The Election being ended, up rose Member *Ben*,
And thank'd his Electors again and again,
Declaring his favourite Object in View,
Was *Fanatical* Schemes to defeat and subdue.

Then the Cannons did roar, and the Bells they did ring,
And Shouts were re-eccho'd, GOD bless *C——h* and *K——g*;
May *Heaven* protect them, for whilst they unite
Old England may laugh at *Schismatical* Spite.

An Exeter electoral ballad of 1761.

1

The Election for *Exeter's* over we find
Mac Billy was slung, and came *first in behind*
He brandish'd his lath, he cry'd and he swore
To see *Seven* Hundred Votes dwindled to *Four*.

2

On *Monday* the Thirtieth of *March* last at *Noon*
The *Dyer*, Old *Cruxy*, and *A[ndre]w B*[rice]
Sat out in *Post-Wheelbarrows* all, 'tis agreed
To set up *Mac Billy* a Member for *Ide*.

3

But the Sons of Mount *Ida* their Rights to maintain
Rejected their Offer and Bribes with Disdain
And bid them not act like such infamous Tools
For the Freemen of *Ide* hated *B-ns* and *Fools*.

4

Huzzaing for *Billy* and waving his Hat
The next that advanced was *Lord Petulant Flat*
Who swore that Election should not be delay'd
For he was a *Lord*, and he would be obey'd.

5

The honest Electors then boldly reply'd
We are all *Cobleans*, and scorn to change Side
Then for *Morrish* and *Odam* aloud they did bawl
For *Morrish* and *Odam*, Huzza! one and all.

6

To chuse me, says *Mac*, if you do not think fit
I'll ride up to *London*, and get a *New Writ*
A Writ, replies *Morrish*, with a comical Grin
For yourself, I presume, at the Suit of Old *Phin*!

7

The Election being ended, up rose Member Ben
And thank'd his Electors again and again
Declaring his favourite Object in View
Was *Fanatical* Schemes to defeat and subdue.

8

Then the Cannons did roar, and the Bells they did ring
And Shouts were re-echo'd, God Bless C[hurc]h and K[in]g
May *Heaven* protect them, for whilst they unite
Old England may laugh at *Schismatical* Spite.

VERSION 33
'Tam Pearse, Tam Pearse, lend us your Grey Mayor', 1869

This variant was written for and published by *The Dartmouth & South Hams Chronicle* in 1869.[260] It demonstrates the longstanding device of adding personal names in order to enhance the local interest of the song. It is twenty years older than that collected by Baring-Gould. Dartmouth was then in the midst of a controversy over the expenditure of public funds for the improvement of local sanitation. These lines were published with a playful explanation that 'they had a striking resemblance to a much more ancient ballad… the title of which is *Tam Pearse, Tam Pearse, lend us your Grey Mayor*'. For more than a dozen years there were moves within the port to improve sanitation. It had been claimed that 'thick black fluid' commonly flowed beneath the windows of the guildhall and that the majority of the town's 'filth' was cast into the public streets.[261]

1

Bill Rees, Bill Rees, you'll make a brave Mayor
    All along, all along, all along lee
For the Tories and Whigs, Dartmouth honours must share
    With George Bidder, George Lidstone, Jack Hurrell, Sam Lake,
Phil Widdicome, Ash Hawke, Nix Hannaford, Old Uncle Tom Tucker and all!

2

The first thing, Bill Rees, is to make us a Sewer
    All along, all along, all along lee
That we may have Dartmouth both wholesome and pure
    With George Bidder, George Lidstone, Jack Hurrell, Sam Lake,
Phil Widdicome, Ash Hawke, Nix Hannaford, Old Uncle Tom Tucker and all!

3

Where shall we get money to pay for the drain?
    All along, all along, all along lee
Why rate all the poor folks again and again
    With George Bidder, George Lidstone, Jack Hurrell, Sam Lake,
Phil Widdicome, Ash Hawke, Nix Hannaford, Old Uncle Tom Tucker and all!

4

The poor are near gone, and the rich become poor
    All along, all along, all along lee
You'll drain all the cash, till you cannot drain more
    For George Bidder, George Lidstone, Jack Hurrell, Sam Lake,
Phil Widdicome, Ash Hawke, Nix Hannaford, Old Uncle Tom Tucker and all!

5

And how shall we wash out the muck in the drain?
    All along, all along, all along lee
The Resevoy's empty, and it won't always rain
    For George Bidder, George Lidstone, Jack Hurrell, Sam Lake,
Phil Widdicome, Ash Hawke, Nix Hannaford, Old Uncle Tom Tucker and all!

6

Why surely, there can't be of water much lack
    All along, all along, all along lee
If fresh won't go forward, why salt will come back
    To George Bidder, George Lidstone, Jack Hurrell, Sam Lake, Phil Widdicome,
Ash Hawke, Nix Hannaford, Old Uncle Tom Tucker and all!

7

So they made a big rate, and they cut a big trench

    All along, all along, all along lee

And they said they'd get rid of corruption and stench

    Did George Bidder, George Lidstone, Jack Hurrell, Sam Lake, Phil

Widdicome, Ash Hawke, Nix Hannaford, Old Uncle Tom Tucker and all!

VERSION 34
'Budleigh Salterton Railway', 1894

This variant was written and printed by T. Andrews of 15 High Street in Budleigh Salterton.[262] 'Widdicombe Fair' had been adapted and performed in 1894 before 2,000 guests at Bicton for the coming of age celebrations of Miss Rolle. The tune was retained for this parody and there were 'unanimous loud shouts of approval' for the lyrics.[263] A branch railway had been proposed decades earlier and the scheme was resurrected in 1894. There was opposition from commercial interests in Exmouth but the line opened three years later with stops at Tipton St John, Newton Poppleford, East Budleigh, Budleigh Salterton and Littleham.[264] The lines mention two Prime Ministers in William Gladstone and his successor Archibald Primrose, 5th Earl of Rosebery.

1

My friends there's a railway 'll be made, so I'm told

    All along, down along, out to the sea

So shan't be no longer left out in the cold

    From Tipton, droo' Harpford, Newton Poppleford, past Colaton,

East Budleigh

    By Otterton, Budleigh Salterton, Bicton and all!

2

Now some Neighbours have raised up a terrible talk

    All along, down along, out by the Exe

They say us don't want 'un, and can very well walk

    From Tipton, droo' Harpford, Newton Poppleford, past Colaton,

East Budleigh

    By Otterton, Budleigh Salterton, Bicton and all!

3

To the great House of Lords they went and they sweared
    All along, down along, out by the Docks
That at present we're well and conveniently served
    From Exmouth, by Cranford, stop at Halfway, past Liverton, by the
Gravel-pit, down Knowle Hill
    Into Salterton, Budleigh and all!

4

That no faster conveyance than Mortimore's 'bus
    Job along, walk along, crawl along – Stop!
Could be wanted to carry the stoutest of us
    From Exmouth, by Cranford, stop at Halfway, past Liverton, by the
Gravel-pit, down Knowle Hill
    Into Salterton, Budleigh and all!

5

That the Docks and all Tradesmen of Exmouth must fail
    All Along, down along, round by the Strand
When Supplies and our Visitors reach us by rail
    From Tipton, droo' Harpford, Newton Poppleford, past Colaton,
East Budleigh
    By Otterton, Budleigh Salterton, Bicton and all!

6

We should carry, they say, in a week and a half
    All along, down along, over the Line
But a lobster, a goose, two pigs and a calf
    From Tipton, droo' Harpford, Newton Poppleford, past Colaton,
East Budleigh,
    By Otterton, Budleigh Salterton, Bicton and all!

7

Then Lord Roseberry [sic] and Gladstone they ups and they says
    All along, down along, up by the Thames
'Free Trade you must have and a Railway that pays
    From Tipton, droo' Harpford, Newton Poppleford, past Colaton, East Budleigh
    By Otterton, to Budleigh Salterton, Bicton and all!

8

What Exmouth is asking is nought but protection
    All along, go along, fiddle-de-dee
So of a through line, you must make the first section
    From Tipton, droo' Harpford, Newton Poppleford, past Colaton, East Budleigh
    By Otterton, to Budleigh Salterton, Bicton and all!

9

Now when that is made, we don't mean to rest
    All along, out along, down by the sea
For a railway right through will be clearly the best
    From Tipton, droo' Harpford, Newton Poppleford, past Colaton, East Budleigh
    By Otterton, to Budleigh Salterton, Exmouth and all!

(encore verse)

Now if Salterton merchants can't meet the demand
    All along, out along, down by the sea
Why Exmouth can send their coals, sugar and sand
    From Exmouth, by Cranford, stop at Halfway, past Liverton, by Gravel-pit, down Knowle Hill, into Salterton, Bicton and all!

VERSIONS 35a-b
Untitled (Pension Act, 1909)

This political version regarding the Pension Act was written in dialect by A. J. Coles. It appeared in a newspaper feature 'The talk of Uncle Tom Cobleigh' in October 1909.[265] The Act had become law nine months earlier. It awarded five shillings a week to those eligible (over the age of 70 and having an annual income no greater than £31 10s) with seven shillings and six pence for married couples. The dialect version has been translated by Keith Stevens as Version 34b.

Its style can be compared with another political parody written three years earlier which concerned an education bill. It was entitled 'Farmer [Augustine] Birrell's Grey Mare' and had one verse:

> Farmer Birrell went out to the foot of the hill
> > All along, down along, out along lee
> And he seed the grey mare a-making her will
> > With Archbishop, Marquis, London, Salisbury,
> > > Halsbury, Cawdor, Lord Londonderry and all.[266]

VERSION 35a
Untitled (Pension Act, 1909)

1

Varmer Weelyum, jiss 'arken tu wat I du zay
> Aul along, down along, out along lee
I zim yew be gotten tu sebenty thic day
Wi' yewre 'orses, an' carts, an' yewre stock, an' yewre mows An' a plenty ov zavin's an' aul
> Sivvral 'underds tu dray pin an' aul.

2

Wull, wull, me old son, hev'ee yered tha gude noos?
> Aul along, down along, out along lee
Vive shillun' a wick bant sich vurry 'ard doos
Whane tes giv'd ee fer nuthen vrim other vokes' stores
> Twull pay fer yewre baccy an' aul
> An' a drap ov gude sperritts an' aul.

3

Jiss vull-up thic paaper an' sine ee zo wull
    Aul along, down along, out along lee
Yew du knaw yewre awn bizniss, an' zo yew kin tull
That yew dawn arn wan appny be sweat ov yewre brow
    Yew be livin' raytir-ed an' aul
    Son Jan be tha varmer an' aul.

4

My zakes, ther's old missus, us 'ont vergit she!
    Aul along, down along, out along lee
'Er be sebenty tew, as be wull known tu we
'Er shall hev 'er shillun zo wull as 'er man
    My ivvers, tane shillun' in aul!
    Laur massy, tane shillun' in aul!

5

Yew dawn zim tes vitty tu tek aul thic pelf?
    Aul along, down along, out along lee
Ther be uthers as teks mun zo wull as yewreself
    Tes a matter ov swearin', that's aul
    Awnly sweer yew dawn arn nort, that's aul.

6

Wy, yew knaw Groser Tucker tu 'Cacia Lodge!
    Aul along, down along, out along lee
'Aw, ee be a sharp 'un, an' up a dodge
An' ee've got ees old Pinshun wayout ne'er a wurd
    Fer ee dawn arn wan farden at aul
    Wat ee've putt by bant countin' at aul.

7

Ee've cob an' a trap, an' a bewtivul 'ouse
   Aul along, down along, out along lee
An' a darter zo meen 'er wud starvey a mouse
A pehanner, an' furnishure vit fer a lord
    A widder-man ee be an' aul
    Jane be zarvint, 'ousekaper, an' aul.

8

Du'ee luke tu thay Ballsums tu Windycott Varm
   Aul along, down along, out along lee
Vurry pasibul vokes thay, as dawn du no 'arm
But zo miserly near thay begridge ivvry cent
    Thof thay awn ivvery aker an' aul
    Vine medders, gude tillage, an' aul.

9

Wull, missus's muther du bide long ov thay
   Aul along, down along, out along lee
'Er've med auver 'er munny, or zo yokes shid zay
Tull sich taime as 'er jineth 'er man, as 'be dade
    Fer 'er kape, close, an' vittels an' aul
    Dockter's-traade, an' ees 'tendanse an' aul.

10

Aw, wull yew belave I whane I tull ee trew!
   Aul along, down along, out along lee
Thay hev 'plied fer 'er Pinsnun, ees, an' got thic wan tew!
    Nor yew carn't zay no uther at aul
    Sich vokes dawn hev, no conshunse et aul.

11

Did'ee yer ov old Towzer pin larst Pinshun Day!
    Aul along, down along, out along lee
Ee vall'd down in tha aidge-trow pin ees 'omewards way
    Vrim tha Vorester's Arms, where e bided tew long
    Better-waays ee'd no pinshun at aul
    Awnly mekketh ee bastely, that's aul.

12

Zo du'ee mek hay wiles tha sun ee du shine
    Aul along, down along, out along lee
Fer wat's mine's me awn, an' wat's yewres be mine
Zes Asquith, an' Morley, an' Winston, Gus Birrell, Jan Burns, Lloyd Garge.
But-
    Giddout! us wull zay tu thay aul
    Git 'ome! us wull zay tu thay aul.

MORAL

Thay as wants an' daysarves mun pinshuns shall kape
    Aul along, down along, out along lee
Wuther Tory Libral cum tap ov tha hape
But thase hoseburds wi' munny, an' drunken old chaps
    Thay shant heve no pinshuns at aul
    Not wan farden ov pinshun at aul.

Us'll vote fer tha Tories as knaw wat be wat
    Aul along, down along, out along lee
An' wull give tu tha thin wans, an' lave out fat
As hev got a gude plenty, but 'ont tull tha trewth
    Bant sich vules as tu 'elp thay at aul
    Fer thay dawn nade no suckerin' 'taul.

VERSION 35b
Untitled (Pension Act, 1909), 2019

1

Farmer William, just harken to what I do say
    All along, down along, out along lee
I see you be gotten to seventy this day
With your horses and carts and your stock and your cows
    And plenty of savings and all
      Several hundreds to drop in and all.

2

Well, well, my old son, have you heard the good news?
    All along, down along, out along lee
Five Shillings a week isn't such very hard dues
When it is given thee for nothing from other folk's store
    It will pay for your tobacco and all
      And a drop of good spirits and all.

3

Just fill up this paper and sign he so will
    All along, down along, out along lee
You do know your own business, and so you can tell
That you don't earn one ha'penny by sweat of your brow
    You be living retired and all
      Son Jan be the Farmer and all.

4

My Goodness (sakes) there's old Missus, us wont forget she!
    All along, down along, out along lee
Her be seventy two, as be well known to we
Her shall have her shilling so will her man
    My heavens, ten shillings in all
      Lord Mercy, ten shillings in all.

5

You don't see it is fit to take all this wealth?
    All along, down along, out along lee
There be others as take money so well as yourself
    It is a matter of swearing, thats all
    Only swear you don't earn nothing, that's all.

6

Why, you know Grocer Tucker at Acacia Lodge
    All along, down along, out along lee
How he be a sharp one, and up a dodge
And he has got his pension without never a word
    For he don't earn one farthing at all
    What he have put by isn't counting at all.

7

He has a cob and a trap, and a beautiful house
    All along, down along, out along lee
And a daughter so mean she would starve a mouse
A piano, and furniture fit for a lord
    A widower man he be and all
    Jane be servant, housekeeper and all.

8

Do you look to those Ballsums at Windycott Farm
    All along, down along, out along lee
Very passable folks they, as don't do no harm
But so miserly near they begrudge every cent
    Tho they own every acre and all
    Fine meadows, good tillage and all.

9

Well, the wife's mother do abide long with they
    All along, down along, out along lee
Her have made all of her money or so folks should say
Till such time as her joineth her man, as be dead
    For she keep, clothes and food and all
    Doctor's trade, and his attendance and all.

10

Oh, well you believe I want to tell you true
    All along, down along, out along lee
They have applied for her pension, he's and got that one too
    Nor you can't say no other at all
    Such folks don't have, no conscience at all.

11

Did you hear of old Towzer been last Pension Day!
    All along, down along, out along lee
He falled down in the hedge row upon he's homeward way
From the Foresters Arms, where he abided too long
    Better-ways he'd no pension at all
    Only maketh he beastly, that's all.

12

So do you make hay while the sun he do shine
    All along, down along, out along lee
For what's mine's me own, and what's yours be mine
Says Asquith, and Morley, and Winston, Gus Birrell, Jan Burns, Lloyd George, But
    Get out! we will say to them all
    Get home! we will say to them all.

Moral

Those as wants and deserves a pension shall keep

    All along down along out along lee

Whether Tory Liberal come top of the heap

But those hosebirds [rascals] with money and drunken old chaps

    They shan't have no pensions at all

    Not one farthing of pension at all.

Us will vote for the Tories as they know what be what

    All long down alone out along lee

And will give to the thin ones, and leave out fat

As have got a good plenty, but won't tell the truth

    Baint such fools as to help they at all

    For they don't need no suckering at all!

VERSION 36
'A Biddiscombe Mayor', 1904

This anonymous parody in four verses concerned councillors who were investigating the possibility of altering the form of local government in Willesden, north-west London. In 1904 each of the men noted in the first verse were councillors who had voted to become independent while those in the second verse had voted against. Willesden's first mayor took office in 1933.[267]

1

Charlie Pinkham, Charlie Pinkham, woulds't laike to be Mayor?

    All along, out along, down along lea

Charlie Biddiscombe wants a red robe fur tu wear

    And so du Frank Hilborn, Dave Barrett, Harry Alford, George Johnson, Jack Jones, Harry Kidgell, Will Dunn, Stevey Hodnett,

    Old Uncle Malachi an' all.

2

Says he, *it baint gude enow fur chaps tu the West*
   All along, out along, down along lea
How mun we be better wi' cocked hats tu be dressed?
   And so said Jim Adams, Will Riley, Will Pincombe, Ben Griffin, Jimmy Bate,
   Albert Gale and our Jonathan an' all.

3

Hev some lollipops, and let that there golden chain bide
   All along, out along, down along lea
But to wear that cocked hat there were many who sighed
   Michael Kelly, Jim Perkins, Harry Fry, Joe Shenann, Charlie Cowley,
Ted Hunt,
   And President Butteries an' all.

4

So they put un tu parish, but fegs twadn't passed
   All along, out along, down along lea
No money in that guarantee bag was cast
   So Lord Mayors aint Georgie Sexton, Charlie Biddiscombe, Dave Barrett,
   Nor John Smith of Stonebridge an' all.

VERSION 37
'Us Favours Jan Spear', 1910

These seven verses were written to support John Spear, the parliamentary candidate for the Conservative Party at Tavistock.[268] They describe him as 'Honest Jan'. An unidentified staff journalist wrote the lines for the *Western Morning News* and they appeared four days before the election. Spear was unsuccessful. Those individuals mentioned in the parody with Spear were Herbert Henry Asquith (Liberal MP, East Fife, & Prime Minister), Arthur James Balfour (Conservative MP, City of London), Ernest Fitzroy Morrison-Bell (unsuccessful Liberal Unionist candidate, Ashburton), Joseph Chamberlain (Liberal Unionist MP, West Birmingham), Winston Churchill (Liberal MP, Dundee, & Home Secretary), Henry Duke (Conservative MP, Exeter), David Lloyd George (Liberal MP, Carnarvon, & Chancellor of the Exchequer), Sir John

David Lloyd George in about 1922.

Jackson (Conservative MP, Devonport), Bert Lamb (unsuccessful Liberal candidate, Rochester), Sir Henry Lopes (unsuccessful Conservative candidate, Torquay) and H. Barrett Saymour. This parody partly revolves around the issue of tariff reform; the Tariff Reform League argued for protection from unfair foreign imports and advocating preference to dominions and colonies in the Empire. This version also referred to the naval race between Germany and Britain which had been in operation for a decade. In 1906 there had been another election song composed at Tavistock.[269]

1

Jan Spear, honest Jan, cum arken to we
   All along, out along, down along lea
Us wants ee to go to Parlementee
   With Hal Lopes, H. Duke, Cap'en Bell, J. Jackson, Joe Chamberlain
   Chorus Old Arthur James Balfour and all

2

But ow shall I get een to Parliayment
   All along, out along, down along lea
For some of 'em wants H. Luttrell sent
   With Lloyd George, H. Barrett Saymour, Winnie Churchill, Bert Lamb
   Chorus Radeccal Asquith and all

3

When Wednesday comes and our gurt polling day
   All along, out along, down along lea
Us, 'all support ee for sartin, ees fay
   With Hal Lopes, H. Duke, Cap'en Bell, J. Jackson, Joe Chamberlain
   Chorus Old Arthur James Balfour and all

4

For us don't want that old budgit again
   All along, out along, down along lea
Tariff Reform is the right horse to win
   With Jan Spear, Hal Lopes, H. Duke, J. Jackson, Joe Chamberlain
   Chorus Old Arthur James Balfour and all

5

Of course, us du want a fust rate navee
　　All along, out along, down along lea
Tu kaip the furriners from conquering and beating of we
　　With Lloyd George, H. Barrett Saymour, Wine Churchill, Bert Lamb
　　Chorus Radeccal Asquith and all.

6

Gude old Chas. Beresford 'ul taache us that game
　　All along, out along, down along lea
So if us doant back un 'twill be a gurt shame
　　With Jan Spear, Hal Lopes, H. Duke, J. Jackson, Joe Chamberlain
　　Chorus Old Arthur James Balfour and all.

7

For our land, our trade, we must all sit tight
　　All along, out along, down along lea
So us 'all kaip England protected quite
　　With Jan Spear, Hal Lopes, H. Duke, J. Jackson, Joe Chamberlain
　　Chorus Old Arthur James Balfour and all.

VERSION 38
'Westminster Fair', 1910

In March 1910 the ballad was recast by B. Simmons as 'Westminster Fair' to support the new Liberal government which had been elected a few weeks before. It was printed in *The South Bucks Standard* and noted as a political parody.[270] The individuals in the company comprised Herbert Henry Asquith (Liberal MP, East Fife, & Prime Minister), John Burns (President of the Local Government Board), Winston Churchill (Liberal MP, Dundee, & Home Secretary), Charles Masterman (Liberal MP, West Ham North) and John Redmond (elected unopposed MP, Irish Parliamentary Party, Waterford). Georgie was most likely David Lloyd George (Liberal MP, Carnarvon, & Chancellor of the Exchequer).

1

John Bull, John Bull, lend us your grey mare
   All along, down along, out along lea
Says Asquith for I'm going to Westminster Fair
   With dear Winnie, and Georgie and John Burns and Masterman
   With Mr John Redmond and all
   With Mr John Redmond and all.

2

And when shall I see again my grey mare
   All along, down along, out along lea
On Friday 'tis sent when in Parliament
   Are dear Winnie and Georgie and John Burns and Masterman
   With Mr John Redmond and all
   With Mr John Redmond and all.

3

Then Friday came, and Saturday noon
   All along, down along, out along lea
But John Bull's grey mare had not trotted home
   With dear Winnie and Georgie and John Burns and Masterman
   With Asquith and Redmond and all
   With Asquith and Redmond and all.

4

So John Bull he went out, and searched all that night
   All along, down along, out along lea
Till down in the valley, he saw a great fight
   Between Winnie and George and John Burns and Masterman
   With Asquith and Redmond and all
   With Asquith and Redmond and all.

5

Then John at last at the truth did arrive
When there his wrecked cart of State he did see
They were all disputing as to which should drive
    Were dear Winnie and Georgie and John Burns and Masterman
    With Asquith and Redmond and all
    With Asquith and Redmond and all.

6

But though John Bull has left them in this horrid plight
Folks who are crossing the moors say they see
Ghostly figures engaged in a terrible fight
    Ghost of Winnie and George and John Burns and Masterman
    With Asquith and Redmond and all
    With Asquith and Redmond and all.

VERSION 39
Untitled (Liberal Party electoral), 1910

These verses appeared seven days before the election in Barnstaple which was held on 27 January 1910 and were written by J. B. of Bratton Fleming to support Sir Ernest Joseph Soares, the Liberal Party candidate. He was successful. The other men mentioned were Herbert Henry Asquith (Liberal MP, East Fife, & Prime Minister), George Borwick (unsuccessful Conservative candidate, Barnstaple), Winston Churchill (Liberal MP, Dundee, & Home Secretary), David Lloyd George (Liberal MP, Carnarvon, & Chancellor of the Exchequer), Richard Haldane (Liberal MP, Haddingtonshire & Secretary of State for War), Henry Petty-Fitzmaurice, 5th Marquess of Lansdowne (leader of the Liberal Unionists, House of Lords). Old Joey was most likely Joseph Chamberlain (Liberal Unionist MP, West Birmingham) and 'Son' Austen may have been his son Sir Joseph Austen Chamberlain (Liberal Unionist MP, East Worcestershire). 'Prince Arthur' was Arthur James Balfour (Conservative MP, City of London). The tune was noted as being 'Widdicombe Fair'.[271]

1

For Lloyd George, for Lloyd George, we'll give three lusty cheers
He'll lead us to vict'ry whatever befall
Beloved of the People and feared by the Peers
Food taxers, scaremongers, dukes, landlords, and brewers
   Our David's a match for them all
Chorus: Our David's a match for them all.

2

We want taxes on land and on wealth that's unearned
For this common sense justice we've long had to wait
And the hardship in this we have not yet discerned
That of wealth that is made by the labour of all men
   One fifth should go back to the State
   Our David's a match for them all.

3

We're delighted to hear what you Tories would tax
You've told us so often the foreigner pays
If so, don't you think you were just a bit lax
Old Joey, son Austen, *Prince* Arthur, etc.
   To let him off bacon and maize?
   Our David's a match for them all.

4

We hear that you've made it the first of your planks
To put up the price of bread, butter, and meat
Do you think from the people you'll get their best thanks
Old Joey, son Austen, *Prince* Arthur, etc.
   For taxing the food that they eat?
   Our David's a match for them all.

5

And now, if the verdict in store you would know
The people are rousing at Liberty's call
With your rotten old planks to the bottom you'll go
Lord Lansdowne, son Austen, *Prince* Arthur, etc.
    Alas, poor old Borwick and all
    Our David's a match for them all.

6

E. J. S., tried and, trusted, is North Devon's true friend
Good-bye and good luck to you, Mr G. B.
For back to St Stephen's [Hall] we'll certainly send
Lloyd George, Mr Asquith, dear Winston, and Haldane
    And, of course, E: J. S. *our* M.P.

VERSION 40
'Proscription Carol', 1921

This variant satirised reorganisation and in-fighting in the British left following the establishment of the Communist Party of Great Britain in 1920. By that date the Fabian Society, the British socialist organisation, had been in existence for more than a generation and in 1915 the National Guilds League was formed by G. D. H. Cole (named in the satirical lyrics) who published this version. The first verse referenced a third group of leading socialists. This variant substituted the name of Tom Pearce with Ned Pease; Edward R. Pease was a founding member of the Fabian Society and a former general secretary. It was published in a collection of songs entitled *The Bolo Book*; Bolo Pasha, a Frenchman, had been executed two years earlier as a German spy and the book mocked the assertion that members of the left not signed up to communism were traitors.

The tune had been used the previous year during a revue of the Fabian Summer School at Godalming.[272] This 'forbidden carol' was probably written by Maurice Reckitt, a Christian socialist known for composing verses. His wife was from Devon. The printed edition of the ballad noted that the lyrics came from 'The Homeland of Mystery', some of which was composed by Reckitt. The tune was that of 'Widdecombe Fair' and it was noted that 'Further stanzas can be devised *ab lib* according to the

161

Ellen Wilkinson who performed in the revue of 1920.

particular company in which the song is being sung.'[273] More than a generation later, in 1956, the ballad was adapted to cite members of the British Communist Party.[274]

1

Friend Lenin has warned us we first must proscribe
Peace upon earth and goodwill towards men
All renegades of the Socialist tribe
Such as [Arthur] Henderson, [J. R.] Clynes, Will Thorne, Philip Snowden,
Ethel Snowden, Jimmie Thomas and Ramsay MacDonald and all
James Ramsay MacDonald and all.

2

Ned Pease, Ned Pease, shall lend us his list
Peace upon earth and goodwill towards men
We need to make sure that no Fabian is missed
Such as [James Joseph] Mallon, Emil Davies, Lawson Dodd, Haden Guest,
Susan Lawrence, Bernard Shaw,
and Beatrice and Sidney [Webb] and all
Dear Beatrice and Sidney and all.

3

Then most of the Guildsmen deserve to be dead
Peace upon earth and goodwill towards men
So let armies of Communists cut off the head
Of Sam Hobson, Mrs [E. C.] Ewer, Maurice Reckitt,
Page Arnot, Douglas Cole, Margaret Cole,
[Alfred Richard] Orage, Major Douglas and all
O God, Major [Clifford Hugh] Douglas and all.

VERSION 41
'The Processional', 1936

Two parodies were written about Golders Green, the north London suburb. One concerned The Golders Green Parliament, a debating society which ran from at least 1914 to 1939.[275] In 1925 it was reported[276] that there was 'a delightfully topical parody' on 'Widdicombe Fair.' One verse reads:

The Golders Green Parliament meets every week
    Up along, come along, look in see
If you're hen-pecked at home you can go there and speak
Says the Liberals, the Tories, the Labours, the Wobblers
    Old Uncle A, "Someone" and all
    Old Uncle A, "Someone" and all.

Eleven years later there was a second parody. It was reported that at a social meeting of the Chamber of Commerce in the City Livery Club in Golders Green:[277]

'The hit of the evening was undoubtedly made by Mr Sutton in a delightful rendering of a local version of Widdicombe Fair, specially written for the occasion by Mr A. W. Lewis, who combines the duties of Hon. Treasurer and social secretary with the post of poet to the Chamber, unlicensed. Waiving his claim to the copyright, Mr Lewis has given me permission to reproduce his lyric, and I do so in the hope that it will be cut out and kept for future use. There is no need to know any dialect in order to sing it, but a little dash of *pure Golders Green* gives it added flavour'.

The Ginger Group was a collection of individuals who had set themselves up as a small active body within a larger group. The individuals named were members of the Chamber of Commerce.

1

Joe Pearce, Joe Pearce, lend me your grey mare
To join a procession in Hendon somewhere
For I'm sure all the Ginger Group Boys will be there
    Harry Finch, Bunny Watts, Charlie Landau,
Willie Somers, Henry Shannon and Uncle Bob Seabrook and all
    And Uncle Bob Seabrook and all.

2

The Procession had started and well on its way
With everyone dressed in their brightest array
While perched on a stagecoach all merry and gay
    With Harry Finch, Bunny Watts, Charlie Landau,
Willie Somers, Henry Shannon and Uncle Bob Seabrook and all
    And Uncle Bob Seabrook and all.

3

The Procession, the finest for many a year
Went all round the Parish and when home it drew near
The band couldn't play, they were full up with beer
    Harry Finch, Bunny Watts, Charlie Landau,
Willie Somers, Henry Shannon and Uncle Bob Seabrook and all
    And Uncle Bob Seabrook and all.

4

When it reached the Town Hall, I am pleased to relate
There on the balcony sat in great state
The Mayor and the Councillors, they had just raised the rate
    His Worship the Mayor, Alderman Reynolds, Alderman Clemens,
Alderman Copestake, Brother Ross and Uncle great Scott there and all
    And Uncle great Scott there and all.

5

Golden Green led the way on that festive occasion,
For they did such good work without much persuasion.
So we'll come to the front for next May Coronation,
    With Harry Finch, Bunny Watts, Charlie Landau,
Willie Somers, Henry Shannon and Uncle Bob Seabrook and all
    And Uncle Bob Seabrook and all.

VERSION 42
Untitled (Bedfordshire), 1951

This parody appeared in *The Bedfordshire Times & Independent Standard* following the election of 25 October 1951 in which the Labour Government lost to the Conservatives. In Devon all constituencies were won by the Conservatives except for Plymouth Devonport where Michael Foot won for Labour. 'E. W.' prefaced his version with a note that:

> The other night I dreamed that I had been to Widdicombe Fair, and on my way home across lonely Dartmoor I saw the legendary Tom Pearce and his mare. Instead of Uncle Tom Cobley and all, he had several members of the cabinet around him, and this is what happened.[278]

The six Labour politicians listed in the first four verses (Hugh Dalton, Minister of Local Government and Planning; John Strachey, Secretary State for War; Manny Shinwell, Minister of Defence; Hartley Shawcross, President of the Board of Trade; Hugh Gaitskell, Chancellor of the Exchequer; Clement Atlee, Prime Minister) gave way to the five Conservatives named in the final verse (Winston Churchill, Prime Minister; Christopher Soames, MP, Bedford; Anthony Eden, Foreign Secretary; Maxwell Fyfe, Home Secretary) as well as to 'The Radio Doctor'. This was Charles Hill, later Baron Hill of Luton, Conservative MP. Hill was a medical doctor and during the Second World War had broadcast on the BBC for the Ministry of Food's programme 'Kitchen Front'. There were then restrictions on medical professionals using their own names therefore Hill broadcast as 'The Radio Doctor'.

1

Tom Pearce, Tom Pearce, lend us your grey mare
The House is dividing, we must get there
We're lost upon Dartmoor, and haven't a 'pair'
    Hugh Dalton, John Strachey, Manny Shinwell, Hartley Shawcross,
Hugh Gaitskell.
    Old Uncle Clem Attlee and all.

2

Now why should lend you my little grey mare?
What good could it do, if you did get back there?
I think I'll just leave you to stay here and swear
    With Hugh Dalton, John Strachey, Manny Shinwell, Hartley Shawcross,
Hugh Gaitskell
    Old Uncle Clem Attlee and all.

3

And so o'er the moor through the cold of the night
They followed their leader, a pitiful sight!
Whilst the Commons divided, not to Left, but to Right
    Without Dalton, or Strachey, Manny Shinwell, Hartley Shawcross,
Hugh Gaitskell
    Old Uncle Clem Attlee and all.

4

And so to the country they all had to go
And the people without hesitation did throw
Right out their necks in the cold winter snow
    Hugh Dalton, John Strachey, Manny Shinwell, Hartley Shawcross,
Hugh Gaitskell
    Old Uncle Clem Attlee and all.

5

So thanks to Tom Pearce our worry now o'er is
The old gang is squashed and the country once more is
Well governed and cared for and led by the Tories
    With Winston Churchill, Christopher Soames, Anthony Eden, Maxwell Fyfe
    And the Radio Doctor and all.

FOREIGN LANGUAGES

Translations of 'Widdicombe Fair' have been made in Spanish, French and Italian. In the 1930s an English traveller also concocted a version while in Tetuan. He included

Moroccan figures in the chorus and while he sang in English his Moroccan hosts sang in Arabic. It was, he thought, an astonishing chorus of 'Sīdi Moulai Idrīs, Ramzaymacdonall'd, Uncle H'tom Kobbelei and all'.[279]

VERSIONS 43a-b
Untitled (Spanish), 1931

This parody, in twelve verses, was translated into Argentinian Spanish in 1931 by Jerónimo del Rey, the pseudonym of Leonardo Castellani.[280] Castellani was an Argentinian priest and writer who took his edition from *The Oxford Songbook*.[281] It has been translated by Professor Richard Hitchcock and entitled 'Arnaldo, Carchín and All'.

VERSION 43a
Untitled (Spanish), 1931

1

Don Babel Manitto, Don Babel Manitto
¡mañanῃita fresca y rabona!
Me presta el vejo mancarrón un ratito
a mí, a Areo, al Gringo y Carlos Castellani,
Celestino Lenteri, Luis Duriú, Manuel Roselli,
con Armando Darán, el Chalchut Pisech y todos
con Arnaldo, Carchín y todos?
¡con Arnaldo, Carchín y todos!

2

Don Babel Manitto está sordo y con su guitarra
¡manañita fresca y rabona!
Saltemos por atrás el cerco y le echamos garra
conmigo, con Areo, el Gringo y Carlos Castellani,
Celestino Lanteri, Luis Duriu, Manuel Roselli,
con Armando Darán, el Chalchut Pisech y todos
con Arnaldo, Carchín y todos?
¡con Arnaldo, Carchín y todos!

3

El viejo flete que fue caballo de carrera...
¡mañanita fresca y rabona!
Se emborracha de golpe de niñez y montonera
como yo, y Areo, el Gringo y Carlos Castellani,
Celestino Lanteri, Luis Duriu, Manuel Roselli...
con Armando Darán, el Chalchut Pisech y todos
con Arnaldo, Carchín y todos?
¡con Arnaldo, Carchín y todos!

4

Don Babel va a salir a caballo al caer el día...
no lo encuentra al bicho y va corriendo a la policía
por causa mia, y Areo, el Gringo y Carlos Castellani,
Celestino Lanteri, Luis Duriu, Manuel Roselli,
El viejo pingo dispara como un Diablo al Puerto...

5

En mitad del camino da un relincho y cae muerto
conmigo, con Areo, el Gringo y Carlos Castellancon Armando Darán,
el Chalchut Pisech y todos
con Arnaldo, Carchín y todos?
¡con Arnaldo, Carchín y todos!

6

El sargento Cleto sale en comisión y dos soldados...
¡Las mamás miedosas le hacen encargos desolados!
para mí, Areo, el Gringo y Carlos Castellani,
Celestino Lanteri, Luis Duriu, Manuel Roselli,
con Armando Darán, el Chalchut Pisech y todos
con Arnaldo, Carchín y todos?
¡con Arnaldo, Carchín y todos!

7

Es de noche, el río crecido y en medio el camino al puerto
me encuentran llorando de miedo y un caballo muerto
con Areo, y Carlos Castellani
Celestino Lanteri, Luis Duriu, Manuel Roselli,
con Armando Darán, el Chalchut Pisech y todos
con Arnaldo, Carchín y todos?
¡con Arnaldo, Carchín y todos!

8

Qué coscorrón me dio el sargento y tirón de oreja...!
Y a la cafúa a bombear agua con la bomba vieja
con Areo y Carlos Castellani
Celestino Lanteri, Luis Duriu, Manuel Roselli,
con Armando Darán, el Chalchut Pisech y todos
con Arnaldo, Carchín y todos?
¡con Arnaldo, Carchín y todos!

9

Pero no paró así no más el terrible asunto...,
de la gran rabona y el robo y el flete difunto
con Areo, el Gringo y Carlos Castellani,
Celestino Lanteri, Luis Duriu, Manuel Roselli,
con Armando Darán, el Chalchut Pisech y todos
¡con Arnaldo, Carchín y todos?
con Arnaldo, Carchín y todos!

10

Cuaundo el largo invierno desata su huracán sombrio...
despierto asustado de noche, llueve y hace frío
con Areo, el Gringo y Carlos Castellani,
Celestino Lanteri, Luis Duriu, Manuel Roselli,
con Armando Darán, el Chalchut Pisech y todos,
con Arnaldo, Carchín y todos?
¡con Arnaldo, Carchín y todos!

11

El fantasma del ánima en pena del caballo reventado
dispara por las calles del pueblo common un condenado
con Area, el Gringo y Carlos Castellani,
Celestino Lanteri, Luis Duriu, Manuel Roselli,
con Armando Darán, el Chalchut Pisech y todos
con Arnaldo, Carchín y todos?
¡con Arnaldo, Carchín y todos!

12

Esta historia horrenda y verdica, caros niños, demuestra
No hay querobar caballos viejos sin permison de la maestra
ni juntarse con Areo, el Gringo y Carlos Castellani,
Celestino Lanteri, Luis Duriu, Manuel Roselli,
con Armando Darán, el Chalchut Pisech y todos
con Arnaldo, Carchín y todos?
¡con Arnaldo, Carchín y todos!

VERSION 43b
'Arnaldo, Carchin and All', 2019

1

Don Babel Manitto, Don Babel Manitto
On this bright and breezy morning!
Lend me your old nag for a while
To me and to Areo, the Yank and Carlos Castellani, Celestino Lanteri, Luis
Duriu, Manuel Roselli, with Armando Daran, the Chalchut Pisech and all,
 With Arnaldo, Carchin and all?
 With Arnaldo, Carchin and all!

2

Don Babel Manitto is deaf and playing his guitar
On this bright and breezy morning!
We jump over the fence from the back and seize the horse
I do, with Areo, the Yank and Carlos Castellani, Celestino Lanteri, Luis Duriu,
Manuel Roselli, with Armando Daran, the Chalchut Pisech and all,

With Arnaldo, Carchin and all?
With Arnaldo, Carchin and all!

3

This old nag which belonged to Carrera…
On this bright and breezy morning!
Quite suddenly becomes skittish and frisky
Like me and Areo, the Yank and Carlos Castellani, Celestino Lanteri, Luis
Duriu, Manuel Roselli, with Armando Daran, the Chalchut Pisech and all
    With Arnaldo, Carchin and all?
    With Arnaldo, Carchin and all!

4

Don Babel wants to go for a ride at nightfall…
He can't find the animal and goes hotfoot to the police
On my account and that of Areo, the Yank and Carlos Castellani,
Calestino Lanteri, Luis Duriu, Manuel Roselli,
The old horse bolts like a bat out of Hell…

5

Halfway there it gives a loud whinny and drops down dead
With me, with Areo, the Yank and Carlos Castellani, Celestino Lanteri, Luis
Duriu, Manuel Roselli, with Armando Daran, the Chalchut Pisech and all
    With Arnaldo, Carchin and all?
    With Arnaldo, Carchin and all!

6

Sergeant Cleto is on the job and two soldiers with him…
Frightened mamas made grief-stricken pleas to the sergeant
On behalf of me, Areo, the Yank and Carlos Castellani, Celestino Lanteri, Luis
Duriu, Manuel Roselli, with Armando Daran, the Chalchut Pisech and all
    With Arnaldo, Carchin and all?
    With Arnaldo, Carchin and all!

7

It's night-time, the river's in flood and they find me
Halfway to the harbour, weeping in fright with a dead horse beside me
And Areo, the Yank and Carlos Castellani, Celestino Lanteri, Luis Duriu,
Manuel Roselli, with Armando Daran, the Chalchut Pisech and all
    With Arnaldo, Carchin and all?
    With Arnaldo, Carchin and all!

8

The sergeant clouted me over the head and pulled my ear…!
And off to the clink to pump water with the old pump
With Areo, the Yank and Carlos Castellani, Celestino Lanteri, Luis Duriu,
Manuel Roselli, with Armando Daran, the Chalchut Pisech and all
    With Arnaldo, Carchin and all?
    With Arnaldo, Carchin and all!

9

But that was not the end of the terrible affair…
Of the great wheeze, the theft and the dead nag
With Areo, the Yank and Carlos Castellani, Celestino Lanteri, Luis Duriu,
Manuel Roselli, with Armando Daran, the Chalchut Pisech and all
    With Arnaldo, Carchin and all?
    With Arnaldo, Carchin and all!

10

When the long winter unleashes its dismal hurricane
I suddenly wake up in the night, when it's cold and raining outside
With Areo, the Yank and Carlos Castellani, Celestino Lanteri, Luis Duriu,
Manuel Roselli, with Armando Daran, the Chalchut Pisech and all
    With Arnaldo, Carchin and all?
    With Arnaldo, Carchin and all!

11

The ghost of the horse's soul in torment
Bolts thorough the streets like one condemned
With Areo, the Yank and Carlos Castellani, Celestino Lanteri, Luis Duriu,
Manuel Roselli, with Armando Daran, the Chalchut Pisech and all
    With Arnaldo, Carchin and all?
    With Arnaldo, Carchin and all!

12

Dear children, this tale, terrible but true, tells us
That we must not steal old horses without teacher's permission
Nor should we consort with Areo, the Yank and Carlos Castellani, Celestino
Lanteri, Luis Duriu, Manuel Roselli, with Armando Daran, the Chalchut Pisech
and all
    With Arnaldo, Carchin and all?
    With Arnaldo, Carchin and all!

VERSION 44
'La foire de Widdicombe', 1940

In 1940 Félix Rose translated 'Widdicombe Fair' for his *Les Grands Lyriques Anglais*, an anthology of verse in the English language.[282] The book was published in Paris in May, only a few weeks before the German occupation. One reviewer commented that 'Anglo-French cooperation and understanding on the intellectual side could not have been better served'. Rose lived in England during at least part of the war.[283] His translation has some oddities including the use of 'Cobley et cetera' as 'and the rest' or 'and so on' instead of *'et tout'* or *'et tous les autres'* for 'and all'.

1

Tom Pearse, Tom Pearse, prête-moi ta jument noire
    Hue oh, hey oh, hey hue donc de là
Car à Widdicombe J'irais à la foire
    Avec Bill Brewer, Jan Stewer, Peter Gurney, Peter Davey, Dan Whiddon,
Harry Hawk
    Oncle Tom Cobbleigh et cœtera
    Oncle Tom Cobbleigh et cœtera.

The French version was printed shortly before the Germans occupied Paris in 1940.

2

– Et quand reverrai-je ma bonne jument noire?
   Hue oh, hey oh, hey hue donc de là
– Vendredi matin ou samedi soir!...
   Avec Bill Brewer, Jan Stewer, Peter Gurney, Peter Davey, Dan Whiddon,
Harry Hawk
    Oncle Tom Cobbleigh et cœtera
    Oncle Tom Cobbleigh et cœtera.

3

Vint vendredi matin, puis samedi soir
   Hue oh, hey oh, hey hue donc de là
Mais chez Tom Pearse, point de jument noire
   Ni de Bill Brewer, Jan Stewer, Peter Gurney, Peter Davey, Dan Whiddon,
Harry Haw.
    Oncle Tom Cobbleigh et cœtera
    Oncle Tom Cobbleigh et cœtera.

4

Tom Pearse monte sur le plateau, inquiet de sa jument
   Hue oh, hey oh, hey hue donc de là
La voit dans la plaine faisant son testament
   Avec Bill Brewer, Jan Stewer, Peter Gurney, Peter Davey, Dan Whiddon,
Harry Hawk
    Oncle Tom Cobbleigh et cœtera
    Oncle Tom Cobbleigh et cœtera.

5

C'te pauvre vieille jument, la v'là qui trépasse!
   Hue oh, hey oh, hey hue donc de là
Et Tom effrondré pleure comme une lavasse
   Avec Bill Brewer, Jan Stewer, Peter Gurney, Peter Davey, Dan Whiddon,
Harry Hawk
    Oncle Tom Cobbleigh et cœtera
    Oncle Tom Cobbleigh et cœtera.

6

Mais ce n'est pas la fin de l'affreuse affaire
  Hue oh, hey oh, hey hue donc de là
Ni, - bien qu'ils soient morts -, de l'horrible carrière
  De Bill Brewer, Jan Stewer, Peter Gurney, Peter Davey, Dan Whiddon,
Harry Hawk
  Oncle Tom Cobbleigh et cætera
  Oncle Tom Cobbleigh et cætera.

7

Quand le vent du Nord soufflé sur la lande
  Hue oh, hey oh, hey hue donc de là
La vieille jument noire apparaît, toute blanche
  Avec Bill Brewer, Jan Stewer, Peter Gurney, Peter Davey, Dan Whiddon,
Harry Hawk
  Oncle Tom Cobbleigh et cætera
  Oncle Tom Cobbleigh et cætera.

8

Alors on entend pendant toute la nuit
  Hue oh, hey oh, hey hue donc de là
Les os de la jument qui font un très grand bruit
  Et ceux de Bill Brewer, Jan Stewer, Peter Gurney, Peter Davey, Dan Whiddon,
Harry Hawk
  Oncle Tom Cobbleigh et cætera
  Oncle Tom Cobbleigh et cætera.

VERSION 45
Untitled (Italian), 2011

These two verses were translated into Italian by Sir Patrick Leigh Fermor and appeared as part of his funeral service in 2011. Fermor had sung the ballad in Italian to members of the Greek Resistance in Crete during the Second World War. He, along with W. Stanley Moss, famously abducted a German general. The Duchess of Devonshire was fond of Fermor's version and regarded him as 'handsome, funny, energetic and original, he is a brilliant, shining star'. Two decades after his experiences on Crete, in

1960, Fermor visited the Spreyton grave of Tom Cobley. In 1993 a BBC2 play, 'Femme Fatale', included children singing 'Widdicombe Fair' in Italian.[284]

1

Tomaso Pearce, Tomaso Pearce, prestami tua griggia giumenta
Tutti lungo, fuori lungo, giu lungo prato
Perche voglio andare alla fierra di Widdecombe
Con Guilliermo Brewer, Giacopo Stewer,
Pietro Gurney, Pietro Davey,
Daniele Whitton, Enrico Hawke.
Ed il vecchio zio Tomaso Cobbley, e tutti quanti
Ed il vecchio zio Tomaso Cobbley, e tutti quanti

Patrick Leigh Fermor (bottom middle) on the island of Crete during the Second World War with Grigori to his right and W. Stanley Moss to his left.

2

Ma non e terminato quest' affare spaventoso

Tutti lungo, fuori lungo, gui lungo prato

E. benche sono morti, della carriera orrible

Di Guilliermo Brewer, Giacopo Stewer,

Pietro Gurney, Pietro Davey,

Daniele Whitton, Enrico Hawke.

Ed il vecchio zio Tomaso Cobbley, e tutti quanti

Ed il vecchio zio Tomaso Cobbley, e tutti quanti

MISCELLANEOUS

VERSION 46
'Summer Sledging in Sledgometer Verse', 1903

This version was written by *Vox Asini*, the 'voice of the ass', for *The South Polar Times* in 1903. This shipboard newspaper was written by the men with the British National Antarctic Expedition on-board the *Discovery* led by Robert Falcon Scott from 1901 to 1904. The tune was given as being that of 'Widdicombe Fair'.

This was a 'sledging song'; a piece of music intended to aid the men while crossing the snow and ice. Lyrics were motivational, expressed a shared identity and purpose, and used rhyming. Sledging songs drew on the long-established communal singing of sea shanties. In the first verse the officers were introduced, some with nicknames, including the Skipper (Scott), the Pilot (Albert Armitage), Charlie (Charles Royds), Mike (Michael Barnes), Shackles (Ernest Shackleton) and Skellie (Reginald Skelton). The second verse has the scientific staff including Ferrets (Hartley Ferrar), Muggins (Alfred Hodgson), Bunnie (Louise Bernacchi), Billie (Edward Wilson) and Kettles (Reginald Koettlitz). The latter was noted for his length; he stood at more than six feet. There were nearly sixty men on-board the ship and some of the nicknames can be guessed at such as Taff for Thomas Alfred Forster Feather. Eighteen dogs are named or referred to in the lyrics. The verses detailed the trials these men had in attempting scientific research and geographical exploration. The lyrics mention an emperor penguin. Scott was himself a Plymothian: he had been born at Stoke Dameral in 1868.[285]

Seventeen years after the *Discovery* returned to England, Shackleton had a picture of the ballad on-board the ill-fated *Quest* when it sailed from Plymouth for the

Captain Scott in about 1910.

Antarctic in 1921. The song was part of an entertainment for the men while the ship was encased in ice.[286]

1

In the Strait of McMurdo was sledging galore
    All along, out along, down along lee
And we walked on the floe till we came to a shore
    With the Skipper, the Pilot, our Charlie and Mike
    Old Shackles and Skellie and all
    Old Shackles and Skellie and all.

2

There was one to the East'ard and one to the West
    All along, out along, down along lee
One North and one South, and each one was the best
    With the staff scientific and knowledge terrific
    There was Ferrets and Muggins and Bunnie and Billie
    Old Kettles the long'un and all
    Old Kettles the long'un and all.

3

There was others went too and I'll tell you their names
    All along, out along, down along lee
And they worked with their bodies and rested their brains
    For the strain on the Bos'un the long winter through
    And the Engineer too and the Carpenter daily
    And 'Yessir' was awful I know
    I know it was awful I do.

4

Now the way to the South was as plain as a road
    All along, out along, down along lee
And the dogs that went with them went fast as a toad
    And there weren't many more for to lighten the load
    But the Skipper, old Shacks, Billy Wilson, the dogs

There was Nigger, and Jim, Birdie, Brownie and Lewis,
Bos, Bismarck, and Kid, poor old Spud and Fitz-Clarence.
There was Joe from Siberia, a typical sledge dog
Vic, Snatcher, and Stripes, Neil, Gus, Wolf and Grannie
    Old Grannie the pick of 'em all
    Old Grannie the pick of 'em all.

5

And the way to the West was as steep as a stack
    All along, high along, up along lee
And they climbed up the mountains and fell down the cracks
    But they got to the summit and wouldn't have done it
    Except for the Pilot and Skellie and Darby,
    Macfarlane and Taff, Tanky, Walker and Duncan
    McClarke from Ben Nevis and Whitfield and Dell
Croucher, Buckridge and Pilbeam, the Donkey as well
    And indeed I believe that's the lot
    When I add Johno, Ginger and Scott.

6

And the way to the East weren't all honey nor cream
    All along, out along, down along lee
Five days in a blizzard and nowt to be seen
    But a chicken 't may hap, from an Empress' lap
    Though I say it with shame and an egg from the same
    Will bring Bliss to the public at home
    Will bring Bliss to the public at home.

7

And then there was Micky went off for a jaunt
    All along, out along, down along lee
Going nowhere for leather in picnicking weather
    He made a good record with Cre-an the Irishman,
    Bill they call Williamson, Plumley and Smythe,
    Tich, Birdie, Sam Weller and all
    Tich, Birdie, Sam Weller and all.

8

But others there were that went hither and there
    All along, out along, down along lee
'Maggie Murphy' their cocker and 'Plasmon' their fare
With a fraction of biscuit, a portion of cheese
A wee bit o' butter the seal meat to grease
Some sugar, some cocoa, some tea and some fat
Just and odd tin o' milk but you needn't count that
    Well! to name them is more than I dare
    But 'twas 'Plasmon' they lived on I'll swear.

9

And this was the end of the sledging last year
    All along, out along, down along lee
I haven't told all but the rest ye will hear
About Lasho and Cross too, Heald and Hare
For them as loves theories as I love my beer
And this 'bray of an ass' though as brazen as brass
Isn't half so amazin' or quarter as brazen
    As all we shall hear later on
    Of the wonderful things we have done.

VERSION 47
'Fuddlecombe Fair', 1922

In 1922 this variant was collected and printed by the Rucksack Club partly through a need to have an accessible version for use during evenings spent in climbing centres. It was sourced from a collection of George Seatree, a pioneer rock climber.[287] The lyrics mention Tom Pearce but the Grey Mare is transformed into a public house. The company and title have also been replaced with references to alcohol; Jan Dewar (John Dewar) and Johnny Walker (Scotch whiskies), John Power (Irish whiskey) and Billy Bass, Worthington and Guinness (ale and beer). It was noted as being 'Air – Widdicombe Fair (Uncle Tom Cobleigh), G. Major (C)'.

1

Tom Pearce, Tom Pearce, come to the *Grey Mare*
    All along, down along, out along Lee
For I wants for to sample the liquor what's there
    Of Bill Brewer, Jan Dewar, Johnny Walker, Johnny Power, Bew Cannon,
Billy Bass
    Old Worthington, Guinness and all
    Old Worthington, Guinness and all.

2

But when shall I meet 'ee? Afore half-past nine
    All along, down along, out along Lee
And 'ee pay for your drink and I'll pay for mine
    Of Bill Brewer, Jan Dewar, Johnny Walker, Johnny Power, Bew Cannon,
Billy Bass
    Old Worthington, Guinness and all
    Old Worthington, Guinness and all.

3

They climbed to the inn at the top of the hill
    All along, down along, out along Lee
But though they called loudly they got not a gill
    Of Bill Brewer, Jan Dewar, Johnny Walker, Johnny Power, Bew Cannon,
Billy Bass
    Old Worthington, Guinness and all
    Old Worthington, Guinness and all.

4

The whiskey was water, the ale was no more
    All along, down along, out along Lee
And Tom Pearce 'e sat down on a stool and 'e swore
    At Bill Brewer, Jan Dewar, Johnny Walker, Johnny Power, Bew Cannon,
Billy Bass
    Old Worthington, Guinness and all
    Old Worthington, Guinness and all.

5

When the wind bloweth cold on a Saturday night
    All along, down along, out along Lee
Tom Pearce in the *Grey Mare* no more doth delight
    With Bill Brewer, Jan Dewar, Johnny Walker, Johnny Power, Bew Cannon,
Billy Bass
    Old Worthington, Guinness and all
    Old Worthington, Guinness and all.

6

And all the night long we heard groaning instead
    All along, down along, out along Lee
Of Tom Pearce and his mate going thirsty to bed
    Without Bill Brewer, Jan Dewar, Johnny Walker, Johnny Power, Bew Cannon,
Billy Bass
    Old Worthington, Guinness and all
    Old Worthington, Guinness and all.

VERSION 48

'A Song of Steeple Claydon', 1927

This parody was written in 1927 for a Buckingham newspaper. It concerned fundraising efforts to build a recreation ground in Steeple Claydon. It was noted 'air: Widecombe Fair'.[288]

1

Now Claydon folk wanted a ground for their sport
    All along, out along, down along lea
So they hunted around and some money they got
    From George Blake, and George Fearn, Arthur Walter, Frank Walker, Anon
and Sir Harry
    The busy Committee and all
    The busy Committee and all!

2

Three hundred and ninety-six, fifteen and nine
    All along, out along, down along lea
Is cheap for a field so uncommonly fine
    Says George Blake, Messrs. Wigley and Chandley, Fred Jackman, George
Beckett, George Stevens
    The busy Committee and all
    The busy Committee and all!

3

So they paid what they'd got and they borrowed the rest
    All along, out along, down along lea
And they got up two Fetes for to pay off the debt
    Did George Blake, Harry Tompkins, Reg. White, Mrs Walter, Fred Woolhead,
Miss Inns
    The busy Committee and all
    The busy Committee and all!

4

But it wasn't enough, so they struggled along
    All along, out along, down along lea
Getting money for whist and for dancing and song
    With George Blake, Percy White, Billy Quainton, Miss Hawes, Miss Grace,
Mrs Blake
    The busy Committee and all
    The busy Committee and all!

5

And there's only a fiver to finish the score
    All along, out along, down along lea
Next Friday we ought to get that much, and more
    With George Blake, Mr Bingham, Bill Rawlings, Clem Biddlecombe,
Joe Duckmanton
    The busy Committee and all
    The busy Committee and all!

6

In a year and nine months we've collected the lot
    All along, out along, down along lea
And another good hundred we spent on the plot
    With George Blake and Tom Sear, Cyril Keys, Tim Smith, Mrs Ingram,
Miss Manning
        The busy Committee and all
        The busy Committee and all!

VERSION 49
'Verses written after reading a treatise on horse management', 1949

These six verses first appeared in *Punch* in 1949[289] and were subsequently reprinted the following year to advertise the All Ireland Donkey Protection Society and the Worn Out Animal Fund. They pleaded 'for mercy's sake please have these poor faithful creatures shot at home instead at sending them alive abroad'.[290]

Head and shoulders of a cart horse, by James Ward, no date.

1

Tom Pearse, Tom Pearce, lend me your grey mare
    All along, out along, down along lea
Though I know she's the oldest that ever there were
    With Goose Rump, High Croup. Slack Loins, Ewe Neck, Thick Gullet,
Capped Elbow
    And Overshot Fetlock and all, and overshot fetlock and all.

2

I'd lend you my mare with a very good will
    All along, out along, down along lea
Except, she's bin suddenly took very ill
    With Bone Spavin, Bog Spavin, Mallenders, Sallenders, Warbles and Sitfasts
    And Fistulous Withers and all, and Fistulous Withers and all.

3

You'd be only too welcome to her, as I say
    All along, out along, down along, lea
But alas the old girl's in a very bad way
    With cracked Heels, Greasy Legs, Seedy Toe, Poll Evil. Laminitus, Sprung
Hock
    And Springhalt and Quittor and all, and Springhalt and Quittor and all.

4

Well, if you won't lend her I'll buy her instead
    All along, out along, down along, lea
And I'll give you two pounds though she's very near dead
    With Ring Bone, and Side Bone and Big Leg and Colic and Shivering and
Splints
    And Canker and Choking and all, and Canker and Choking and all.

5

I'll take her back home now and put her to bed
  All along, out along, down along lea
And see that she's massaged, anointed and fed
  With Bluestone, Soap Liniment, Boric Acid, Carron Oil, Epsom Salts,
Chloral Hydrate
  And Mustard and Ginger and all, and Mustard and Ginger and all.

6

When she's better I'll show her at Widdicombe Fair
  All along, out along, down along, lea
Dressed up in her best with the greatest of care
  With a Noseband, two Sweat Flaps, Cheek Slip Head,
Rein Hook Studs, Ninth Lancer, Round Lip Strap
  And Billets and Blinkers and all, and Billets and Blinkers and all.

VERSION 50
Untitled (Manchester), 1933

This parody was sung on 17 February 1933 at a dinner of the Manchester Chamber of Commerce in honour of Thomas Dalmahoy Barlow, cotton manufacturer and retiring president of the chamber. It was composed and sung by Fred J. West, vice chairman of the chamber and also chairman of the Manchester Ship Canal Company, who reportedly 'brought the house down'. A dinner companion noted 'West surprised many of us – we didn't suspect him of such hearty yet witty bonhomie.' Neither West or Barlow were Devonians.[291]

The local cotton industry had been in contraction for nearly twenty years because of shrinking sales in overseas markets and the rise of foreign competitors especially those in Japan. However, in 1933 there was some good news: exports to India had increased. The verses refer to the unstable sales ('Dam the Japs') and to the British Empire Economic Conference which had been held at Ottawa in the previous summer and which was responsible for the protection of British manufacturers. Barlow argued that Lancashire would never again 'occupy the happy position of being virtually unchallenged as the principal source of supply for the world's requirements in cotton goods'.[292]

1

Tom Barlow, Tom Barlow, we pledge our esteem
    All along, down along, out along lee
For you've worked mighty hard at the head of our 'team'
    Wi' Dick Bond, Bert Lee, Clare Lees
    Ern Thompson, Ted Streat and
    Old Uncle Fred West and all
    Old Uncle Fred West and all.

2

On many a brave errand has Tom journeyed south
    All along, down along, out along lee
Till the big guns of Whitehall have foamed at the mouth
    At Ted Rhodes, Joe Nall, Bob Graham
    Ken Stewart, Bill Clucas and
    Old Uncle Fred West and all
    Old Uncle Fred West and all.

3

In stemming the tide of depression, perhaps
    All along, down along, out along lee
The likeliest method is Tom's 'Dam the Japs!'
    Wi Bob Irwin, Hal Rodier, Alf Buxton
    Bill Reekie, Jack Boddan, and
    Old Uncle Fred West and all
    Old Uncle Fred West and all.

4

More exports! more exports! is Tom's urgent cry
    All along, down along, out along lee
For cotton can't prosper where idle ships lie
    Wi' Mark Winder, Bill Zimmern, Forrest Hewit,
    Tom Jones, Norman Melland, and
    Old Uncle Fred West and all
    Old Uncle Fred West and all.

5

Now Tom thinks that Hope may from Ottawa spring
    All along, down along, out along lee
But why should Trade's fiddle have only one string
    Wi' Hal King, Ted Sudlow, Bill Sparrow
    Jock Carmichael, Bob Grant, and
    Old Uncle Fred West and all
    Old Uncle Fred West and all.

6

And now that Dick Bond has accepted the onus
    All along, down along, out along lee
He'll foster the spirit Tom Barlow has shown us
    Wi' Dick Bond, Bert Lee, Clare Lees
    Ern Thompson, Ted Streat and
    Old Uncle Fred West and all
    Old Uncle Fred West and all.

VERSION 51
'Widdicombe Fair', 1900

This version, written in prose by E. P. (possibly Eden Philpott), appeared in a national magazine.[293] The writer added details to the story. By dimpsey he or she meant twilight, while mazed means distracted.

"Tom Pearce! come out the house, will 'e? I want thy grey mare this instant moment – caan't wait not a second for un!"

So Tom, he come runnin' out.

'The grey mare,' he said; "why for?"

"Why for should I want un? Doan't 'e know 'tis Widdicombe Fair? Theer's a party of us gwaine, an' I wants your mare for my shay. So be quick, for her be best mare in these paarts us all knaws."

"And' who be along with you, then, so smart an' vitty? By gor! if they doan't all look like gentlefolks in theer flam-new knee breeches!"

"Theer's Bill Brewer – him wi' the red hair an' red-striped west-coat; an' Jan Stewer in parson's auld cast-off small clothes; an' Peter Gurney, from down Tavistock way; an'

Dead horse on a cart, by Thomas Rowlandson.

Peter Davy, as bain't no relation, though the same christening name; an' Harry Hawk, as have jined the Methodists since he got six weeks for poachin'; an' dear auld uncle Tom Cobbleigh, as be eighty-nine years of age, if he isn't a liar, an' idden likely to live to see any more junkettings after this wan; an' a few other chaps also."

"An' when will 'e come home along?" axed Tom Pearce, a bit doubtful like.

"By Friday soon, or Saturday noon," answered the chap; so Tom, he drawed auld mare out the stable an' bargained wi' the merrymakers, an' off they went so gay an' proud as peacocks.

Then the time passed by, an' Friday comed soon, an' Saturday noon; but still theer wasn't no grey mare in sight, an' Tom beginned to grow a bit troubled in his mind, for he knawed what a wild man o' the woods Bill Brewer was out 'pon a spree not to name Jan Stewer, Peter Gurney, Dan'l Whiddon an' Uncle Tom Cobbleigh hisself, who, though a very auld, ancient piece, was so cruel clever and such a tough nut that he'd outlast the youngsters at most fashions o' pleasurin' an' fulishness, an' could drink his stoup along wi' the best.

Mare didn't come home; so Tom Pearce, he went up 'pon top the hill, an' lookin' out along the road to Widdicombe, be gormed if he didn't see the awfulest, shockingest sight ever his eyes fell on! For theer, half a mile off, as it might be, by the side of the road acrost the Moor was his grey mare a makin' her will by the looks of it. For her'd falled down an' was lyin' 'pon the grass; and round her stood Bill Brewer, Jan Stewer, Peter Gurney, Peter Davy, Dan'l Whiddon, Harry Hawk, auld uncle Tom Cobbleigh an' all; an' the intellects of the whole lot of 'em 'peared to be mazed, for they stood around 'an shaked theer stupid heads, an' never a wan of the fules lifted a hand to help the mare.

Tom Pearce, he rinned for his life, awnly to find 'twas tu late to do ought, for auld mare's days was ended, an' her rolled her eyes around an' heaved a gert groan from out her ribs, an' kicked gently wance or twice, then stretched out her neck an' was gone. A gude creature, I assure 'e, as had done her work in the world wi'out no fuss; an' all them grawed men sat down an' cried when her drawed her last breath; an' Tom Pearce he bawled loudest of the lot, as was meet an' right he should – the loss bein' his'n.

Time passed an' so did they men, till theer weern't wan of 'em left above ground; an' now if you please to look in the churchyard nigh to Sticklepath village, wheer most of 'em lived, you can see theer names set out in a row 'pon gude Delabole slates. Auld Uncle Tom Cobbleigh, he was fust to go, an' t'others carried un to his grave; then Harry Hawk – poor twoad got takin' the bettermost folks' hares an' pattridges

Study of a Grey Horse, by Jacques-Laurent Agasse, c1800.

again, an' theer was fightin' an' he had his brains scat abroad; though they gived un Christian burial nowithstandin'. An Jan Stewer went next, an' Bill Brewer close arter un. Then Peter Davy catched a fever along o' gwaine down to Plymouth, an' Dan'l Whiddon died of auld age; an' Peter Gurney, as was the last of 'em, married again when he was seventy-five, an' catched a tartar as polished the poor auld blid off under a twelvemonth.

So that was the end of 'em, as you might think; yet 't wasn't neither, for they hadn't a bin dead more'n a year when a terrible coorious thing happened, an' it comed out as theer was ghosteses 'bout arter dark. Awful doin's, I can tell 'e, an' men, women, an' childer never seed the likes. Fust comed a story as Tom Pearce's auld grey mare had been seen up 'pon top the moor by moonlight. 'Twas the very daps of the creature – awnly gashly white 'stead o' grey; an' her went a loppity lop, just as her did in life, wi' the wind a whistlin', fit to cut your ears off around her, an' the flittermice a flyin' an' the moon-beams a glarin' clean through her ribs! A horrid sight, I warn 'e; an' them as seed it was never the same pussons arter. Grawed, glumpy, an' down-daunted like – as well they might.

Then comed folks tellin' as that weern't all, an' worse remained to see, for a man's ghost be more awesome-like than a beast's, as never doan't do no harm. 'Twas a grandson of Tom Pearce's as seed em fust, a dancin' like scarecrows in the night-wind; an' from what he telled, when he got his breath an' comed round of his fright, theer weern't no room for doubt at all. Them as knawed the parties called home the very faaces of 'em from the words o' Tom Pearce's grandson; 'an 'twas plain as a pikestaff that he'd seen the oneasy spirits of Bill Brewer, Jan Stewer, Peter Gurney, Peter Davy, Dan'l Whiddon, Harry Hawk an' auld uncle Tom Cobbleigh a dancin' an' a prancin' in their grave clothes by night. A proper tantara theer was! An' God-fearin' folk wouldn't pass that way between dimpsy an' cock-light – not for gawlden sovereigns they wouldn't.

So that's how it do stand to this hour; an' if you'm a prayerful soul, wi' faith in the Scriptures, 'tis odds but what you'd see they very ghostes to-morrow night if so be you went up along at the proper moment in a trustful frame of mind. They'll walk till the Judgment, no dout; an' Tom Pearce's auld mare along wi' 'em – like the braave auld song as was writ about it do say:

An' all the long night be heard skirling an' groans

   All along, down along, out along, lee

Wheer Tom Pearce's auld mare be a rattling her bones

   Wi' Bill Brewer, Jan Stewer, Peter Gurney, Peter Davy, Dan'l Whiddon,

Harry Hawk, auld uncle Tom Cobbleigh an' all,

   Auld uncle Tom Cobbleigh an' all.

VERSION 52
'The Terrible Tale of the Somerset Nog', 1967

Kenneth Williams sang this nonsensical and innuendo-laden version as Rambling Syd Rumpo, described as an itinerant folk singer, on the BBC radio programme *Round the Horne*. It was part of a series of such songs; 'a one-note satire on folk revivalists [which] became a tuneful, affectionate send-up of rural dialects and forgotten village customs'.[294] Williams explained in his preamble that his song told the story of a farmer's fabled nog which was borrowed for transportation to the great fair at Ganderpoke Bog. All eighteen of his friends rode the animal except Fat Alice 'who don't get on with no one.' Williams defined a nog as a strange-looking creature being a cross between a nag and a dog, otherwise half Somerset Punch and half dachshund. It stood at three hands high, was eighteen feet long and was 'not pretty to look at but the rhubarb in that part of the world is really magnificent'. The horse died, having snapped in half, and its ghost was afterwards sighted in its divided state. The 'Widdicombe Fair' lyrics had been adapted by Barry Took and Marty Feldman. Their excursionists included Ted Willis, playwright, and Con Mahoney, Head of Light Entertainment.[295]

1

Reg Pubes, Reg Pubes

   Lend me your great Nog

Rollock me pusset and grindle my nodes

For I want for to go to Ganderpoke Bog

   With Len Possett, Tim Screevy, the Reverend Phipps, Peg Leg Loombucket,

Sally Levi, Ginger Epstein, Able Seaman Truefitt, Scotch Lil, Messrs Cattermole,

Mousehabit, Neapthigh and Trusspot (Solicitors and Commisioners for Oaths),

Father Thunderghast, Fat Alice, Con Mahoney, Yeti Rosencrantz, Foo Too

Robinson and Uncle Ted Willis and all

   Poor Uncle Ted Willis and all

2

Reg Pubes, Reg Pubes
   You lent your great Nog
Rollock me pusset and grindle me nodes
And now my remains are in Ganderpoke Bog
   With Len Possett, Tim Screevy, the Reverend Phipps, Peg Leg Loombucket,
Sally Levi, Ginger Epstein, Able Seaman Truefitt, Scotch Lil, Messrs Cattermole,
Mousehabit, Neapthigh and Trusspot (Solicitors and Commisioners for Oaths),
Father Thunderghast, Fat Alice, Con Mahoney, Yeti Rosencrantz, Foo Too
Robinson and Uncle Ted Willis and all
   And Uncle Ted Willis and all

Illustration Sources

Copyright for reproduction rests with or has been determined through private collections, i, xi, 20, 24-8, Pamela Colman Smith, *Widdicombe Fair* (New York, 1899); ii, Sabine Baring Gould, *Songs of the West*, (1892); iii, Yale Center for British Art, B1977.14.354; 3, 6, 20, a private collection; 8-9, *The Sphere*, 24 November, 1906; 14 & 15, private collections; 17, *The Bioscope*, 12 Dec. 1928; 19, Devon Heritage Centre, 5203; 33, a private collection; 36, *The Tatler*, 9 April 1947; 37, a private collection; 44, S. Baring-Gould, *Further Reminiscences, 1864–1894* (1925); 47, Yale Centre for British Art, B1986.29.538; 50-51, a private collection; 53, Yale Center for British Art, B1975.3.1082; 58, Yale Center for British Art, B1977.14.4689; 60, Yale Center for British Art, B1975.4.622; 62, Yale Center for British Art, B2001.2.211; 79, Yale Center for British Art, B2016.10.1; 123 Library of Congress, 201469059; 131, *The Sketch*, 8 Oct. 1941; 139, Devon Heritage Centre, LE 1761/EG2; 155, Library of Congress, 2003668460; 162, Library of Congress, 2016842396; 175, National Archives (USA), 242-HLB-5073-20; 178, courtesy of the estate of William Stanley Moss; 180, Library of Congress, 200963337; 187, Yale Center for British Art, B1977.14.6056; 192, Yale Center for British Art, B1975.3.61; 193, Yale Centre for British Art, B2001.2.155. The map has been drawn by Alan Rosevear.

Abbreviations

BL	British Library
DAT	*Transactions of the Devonshire Association*
DCNQ	*Devon & Cornwall Notes & Queries*
DHC	Devon Heritage Centre
DT	*Daily Telegraph*
E&E	*Express & Echo*
EFP	*Exeter Flying Post*
EPG	*Exeter & Plymouth Gazette*
NDJ	*North Devon Journal*
TG	*Tiverton Gazette*
TWT	*Totnes Weekly Times*
VWML	Vaughan Williams Memorial Library
WDM	*Western Daily Mercury*
WDP	*Western Daily Press*
WG	*Western Gazette*
WMN	*Western Morning News*
WT	*Western Times*

References

1   Sabine Baring-Gould & Henry Fleetwood Sheppard, *Songs of the West* (1889), pt 1; *Herts Advertiser*, 19 March 1898.

2   *Gloucestershire Echo*, 21 Oct. 1950.

3   *EPG*, 20 Dec. 1904; Greatest Hits, The Dance, Say You Will and Time; Hergé, *The Adventures of TinTin* (Boston, 1990 edn), 23.

4   Auberon Waugh, *The Last Word* (Boston, 1980), 180; Anna Russell, *I'm Not Making This Up, You Know* (New York, 1985), 164.

5   *System Product Interpreter User's Guide* (Endicott, New York, 1989), 82.

6   *NDJ*, 14 Feb. 1924; *EPG*, 15 Feb. 1924.

7   *Daily Mail*, 3 Dec. 1964.

8   H. V. Morton, *In Search of England* (1934), 111-113.

9   *Yearbook of the Heather Society* (2001), 40-42; 'Potatos [sic] at Wisley, 1911', *Journal of the Royal Horticultural Society*, XXXVII (1911), 572; *WDP*, 14 Nov. 1922; *WMN*, 27 Oct. 1949; *Hastings & St Leonards Observer*, 18 April 1936; *Kent & Sussex Courier*, 22 Oct. 1937; *Bath Chronicle*, 22 Oct. 1938.

10 Caroline Taggart, *A Classical Education* (2009), 29.

11 The title was changed in the 1905 edition to *Songs of the West, Folk Songs of Devon & Cornwall collected from the Mouths of the People*; *Morning Post*, 22 Nov. 1889.

12 *WDM*, 14 Feb. 1889.

13 Dave Harker, *Fakesong* (1985), 152; Martin Graebe, *As I Walked Out* (Oxford, 2017), 260-1; *WT*, 1 Oct. 1889; *WMN*, 4 & 8 Oct. 1889; *TWT*, 5 Oct. 1889; *EPG*, 9 Oct. 1889; *WDM*, 8, 19 & 26 Nov. 1889; *WMN*, 19 Nov. 1889; *NDJ*, 28 Nov. 1889; *Bideford Weekly Gazette*, 3 & 10 Dec. 1889; *WT*, 7 Dec. 1889; *TWT*, 10 May 1890; *E&E*, 2 June 1890. The ballad was later performed by the Girl Guides to the Princess Royal at Torquay: *Daily Telegraph*, 31 May 1937. It was also sung to the Prince and Princess of Wales in 1909 and to the Prince of Wales in 1924: *DT*, 12 June 1909 & *EPG*, 12 Feb. 1924.

14 Harker, *Fakesong*, 151-2; Sabine Baring-Gould, *Further Reminiscences* (1925), 212-213.

15 *WDM*, 15 March 1889; *TWT*, 23 March 1889; *TG*, 19 Nov. 1889.

16 *WG*, 23 May 1890; *Royal Cornwall Gazette*, 4 Dec. 1890; *Taunton Courier*, 10 Dec. 1890; *Windsor & Eton Express*, 18 July 1891; *Lakes Herald*, 1 Jan. 1892; *Norwich Mercury*, 16 Jan. 1892; *Bridport News*, 4 March 1892; *Dover Express*, 6 Jan. 1893; *Reading Mercury*, 14 Jan. 1893; *Cambridge Independent Press*, 17 Nov. 1893; *Wiltshire Times*, 20 Jan. 1894.

17 *WMN*, 31 July 1920; *DT*, 31 July 1920; *Nottingham Journal*, 13 Feb. 1930; *DT*, 23 Dec. 1967. See also *Parliamentary Debates* (Hansard for 1966), ccxxxii & for 1974, clxxvi.

18   Fred Goss, *Memories of a Stag Harbourer* (1931), 197; Clifton Lisle, *Hobnails and Heather* (New York, 1929), 38.

19   A. J. Davy, 'Widdicombe Fair', *Notes & Queries*, 8th series, XII, 11 Dec. 1897, 475-6; *The Observer*, 4 June 1939; *WDM*, 14 Feb. 1889.

20   *A pictorial and descriptive guide to Dartmoor* (1928), 52.

21   *WMN*, 5 Feb. 1932; *Dundee Evening Telegraph*, 17 Sept. 1936; *WDM*, 17 Nov. 1937; *WT*, 17 June 1936; *Hendon & Finchley Times*; *WDM*, 17 Nov. 1937; 18 Nov. 1938; *NDJ*, 16 Nov. 1950.

22   *Taunton Courier*, 24 April 1901; *NDJ*, 22 March 1906; *Nelson Leader*, 8 May 1931; *The Observer*, 4 June 1939.

23   *Eastbourne Gazette*, 5 April 1905.

24   *Torquay Times*, 22 Oct. 1897.

25   *Evening Telegraph*, 2 March 1936; *WT*, 5 April 1935; *Cornishman*, 6 Nov. 1913.

26   *WT*, 8 June 1889. 'The Devonshire regimental march Uncle Tom Cobley which was arranged by Sergt Major McDermott for the presentation of colours to the regiment at Exeter last year.'; *Yorkshire Evening Post*, 23 Feb. 1907; *Torquay Times*, 16 Sept. 1910; *EPG*, 11 Jan. 1927.

27   *EPG*, 23 Feb. 1927.

28   *Thames Star*, vol. xxx, issue 9118, 12 July 1898; *Western Mail*, 29 Dec. 1949.

29   Gordon West, *By Bus to the Sahara* (1939), 163; John Hunt, *The Ascent of Everest* (1953); John Hunt, '*Victoire sur L'Everest*' in *Gens de Montagne* (1996), 673; Wilfrid Noyce, *South Col* (Melbourne, 1914), 256; W. J. Childs, *Across Asia Minor on Foot* (Edinburgh, 1918), 367; Gordon West, *By Bus to the Sahara* (1939), 163; C. T. Madigan, *Central Australia* (1936), 250.

30   *Cheltenham Chronicle*, 8 May 1915.

31   H. Raymond Smith, *A Soldier's Diary* (1940), 121; *West London Observer*, 22 Nov. 1918.

32   Kenneth E. Kirk, *A Study of Silent Minds* (1918), 45; *EPG*, 11 May 1915 & 31 July 1917; Charles H. Barber, *Besieged in Kut and After* (Edinburgh, 1917).

33   *Derby Daily Telegraph*, 26 July 1915; Peter & Leni Gillman, *The Wildest Dream; the biography of George Mallory* (Seattle, 2000), 153.

34   Joyce Grenfell, *The Time of My Life* (1989), 151; Deborah Devonshire, *Counting My Chickens* (Ebrington, 2002 edn), 155-8; Artemis Cooper, *Patrick Leigh Fermor* (2012), 150-1; Graham Greene, *In Search Of a Character* (New York, 1962), 86.

35   *Portsmouth Evening News*, 7 Nov. 1941; *Clitheroe Advertiser*, 21 Nov. 1941.

36   Graebe, *As I Walked*, 278-82; Penelope Fitzgerald, *The afterlife* (2003), 98.

37   *WMN*, 1 Feb. 1865; *WT*, 9 April 1869; *EPG*, 15 Jan. 1872.

38   *Musical Times*, Vol. 56, No. 874 (1 Dec. 1915), 734; Chamber Ensemble of London, *Over Hill, Over Dale* (2013).

39   Winnifred Atwell, *Around the World in 80 tunes* (1958); Max Harrison, Charles Fox & Eric Thacker, *The Essential Jazz Records* (New York, 1984), 219.

40   Personal communication from Roger Cooper and Ray Phillips, 15 July 2019.

41   *Columbia on Parade* (1932); Burl Ives, *Okeh Presents the Wayfaring Stranger* (1941); *Back in the Day, 50 Children's Favourites* (2012); Jimmie Rodgers, *The Folk Song World of Jimmie Rodgers* (1961); The Nashville Teens, *Rockin' Back to Tobacco Road* (2007); The George Mitchell Minstrels, *On Stage with the George Mitchell Minstrells from the Black and White Minstrel Show* (1962); Jon Pertwee, *Wonderful Childrens Songs* (1972); The King's Singers, *The King's Singers – Lollipops* (1975); The Ionian Singers, *Early One Morning* (1992); Show of Hands, *Cold Frontier* (2001); Professor Arthur C. Throovest, *Album 3* (2011).

42   Harry T. Moore (ed.), *The collected letters of D. H. Lawrence* (Kingswood, 1962), 975; E. Brewster, *D. H. Lawrence* (1931), 276; Richard Perceval Graves, *Robert Graves* (New York, 1987), 81; *The Biographical Edition of the Works of Robert Louis Stevenson* (1895), IV, 299; Patrick Quinn (ed.), *Dictionary of Literary Biography; British Poets of the Great War* (Farmington Hills, 2000), vol. 216, 232.

43   *Hampshire Telegraph*, 2 Feb. 1907.

44   Alec Guinness, *A Positively Final Appearance* (New York, 1999), 9; Agatha Christie, *An Autobiography* (New York, 1977), 303; Peter Cushing, *Past Forgetting* (1988), 35; Nancy Mitford, *Love from Nancy* (Boston, 1993), 189; Melvyn Bragg, *Richard Burton: a life* (1988), 274; Christopher Sykes, *Nancy, The Life of Lady Astor* (New York, 1972), 350; Anthony Thwaite (ed.), *Philip Larkin; Letters to Monica* (2012); P. G. Wodehouse, *Love Among the Chickens* (1920), 105; *Tribune*, 20 Nov. 1959.

45   Constantine FitzGibbon (ed.), *Selected Letters of Dylan Thomas* (1966), 226.

46   Matthew J. C. Hodgart & Mabel P. Worthington, *Song in the Works of James Joyce* (New York, 1959), 97; Rudyard Kipling, *Traffics and Discoveries* (New York, 1904), 158; John Osborne, *Four Plays* (2000), 64-5, 30-1.

47   'Miss M. P. Willcocks as a Novelist', *The Devonian Year Book* (1913), 64-72.

48   *Dorking & Leatherhead Advertiser*, 22 March 1913; *EPG*, 18 Feb. 1913. The original manuscript is owned by the library service in Plymouth: Plymouth & West Devon Record Office, 3180 & 1984.

49   *Worthing Gazette*, 20 Nov. 1929.

50   *New Zealand Herald*, 14 March 1931.

51   'Widecombe Fair in Morocco', *The Devon Year Book*, 1937, 81-2; Philip Thornton, *The Voice of Atlas* (1936), 221-2.

52   *WMN*, 8 Dec. 1930.

53   Baring-Gould, *Songs & Ballads*, xvii; Graebe, *As I Walked*, 121; *Gloucestershire Echo*, 11 March 1936; *Taunton Courier & Western Advertiser*, 9 Oct. 1937.

54   *Petite suite de concert* (New York, 1916), final page; *Catalogue of Music Publications, 1963 supplement* (American Printing House for the Blind, 1963), 6.

55   *NDJ*, 3 Dec. 1907.

56   Thornton, *Voice of Atlas*, 221-2; *The Times*, 14 Sept. 1938.

57   Theo Brown, 'Some Notes on the song *Widecombe Fair*', DCNQ (1952-3), XXV, 167-71.

58   May Byron, 'The burden of the song', *Temple Bar*, Vol. 123, Issue 486 (May, 1901), 43.

59   E. B. Osborn, *Literature and Life* (1921), 196.

60   *EPG*, 7 May 1937; *WT*, 30 March 1899 & 27 Oct. 1905; *EPG*, 31 Dec. 1890; *NDJ*, 13 Jan. 1898.

61   *EPG*, 2 Dec. 1932.

62   *Torquay Times*, 10 May 1895; *E&E*, 21 March 1895.

63   *Eastbourne Gazette*, 8 March 1905.

64   *FT*, 19 Oct. 1994; *EPG*, 16 Jan. 1908 & 13 Nov. 1908; *WT, 10 Dec. 1895; The Cornishman*, 2 March 1911, 28 June 1934 & 25 Jan. 1940; *Bath Chronicle & Weekly Gazette*, 27 April 1940; *WT*, 10 April 1908 & 2 Feb. 1916; *NDJ*, 23 Dec. 1939.

65   *WDM*, 7 Feb. 1928.

66   *South London Press*, 26 Jan. 1889.

67   *Yarmouth Independent*, 1 April 1933; *WG*, 20 Nov. 1931; *Norwood News*, 15 May 1936; *Cornishman*, 9 March 1905; *WDM*, 28 Jan. 1907.

68   *Sunderland Daily Echo & Shipping Gazette*, 13 Jan. 1936.

69   *Birmingham Gazette*, 17 Sept. 1920. See *Sports Special (Green Un)*, 5 Jan. 1929 for another cricket use.

70   J. C. Squire, *Tricks of the Trade* (New York, 1917), 28-9.

71   *Berks & Oxon Advertiser*, 4 Jan. 1907.

72   Peter & Betty Ross (eds), *Marx & Engels Collected Works, Letters, 1856–59* (Moscow, 2010 edn), Vol. 40, 463; *Der Briefwechsel zwischen Friedrich Engels und Karl Marx* (Stuttgart, 1913), II.

73   H. G. Wells, *Travels of a Republican Radical In Search of Hot Water* (1939), 152; Margaret Drabble, *Angus Wilson* (New York, 1995), 53; Len Deighton, *SS-GB* (New York, 1979), 316; Sean O'Casey, *Sunset and Evening Star* (New York, 1955), 214; George Macdonald Fraser, *Royal Flash* (New York, 1970), 214; Catherine Cookson, *The Cinder Path* (Toronto, 1976), 83; John Le Carre, *Tinker, Tailor Soldier, Spy* (1974), 152; Dorothy L. Sayers, *Strong Poison* (1967), 179; Noel Coward, *Pomp and Circumstance* (New York, 1960), 44.

74   Germaine Greer, *Sex and Destiny* (New York, 1984), 465; *Birmingham Daily Post*, 17 March 1973; Joan Collins, *Second Act* (Bath, 1998), 415.

75   *Daily Herald*, 18 Sept. 1931; *Eastbourne Gazette*, 13 May 1914; *Western Mail*, 19 Jan. 1935.

76   *Kent & Sussex Courier*, 1 Nov. 1935.

77   Jules Brown & Mick Sinclair, *Scandinavia* (1993 edn), 442; *The Times*, 17 Feb. 1932; Jack Higgins, *The Eagle Has Landed* (New York, 1975), 93; Gordon Lonsdale, *Spy, Twenty Years in Soviet Secret Service* (New York, 1965), 90.

78   *Birmingham Daily Post*, 9 Oct. 1964.

79   *The Graphic*, 21 Dec. 1929.

80   *London*, Vol. 93, Issue 19 (22 Sept. 1934), 9.

81 Margaret Carill & Sally Burgess (eds), *Publishing Research in English as an Additional Language: Practices, Pathways and Potentials* (Adelaide, 2017), 240-1. See also Alexander P. Sadimenko, 'Organometallic Complexes' in Alan R. Kartizky (ed.), *Advances in Heterocyclic Chemistry*, Vol. 89 (2005), 149.

82 Claude T. Bishop, *How to edit a scientific journal* (Philadelphia, 1984), 26, 134.

83 *The Humorist*, Vol. 21, Issue 526 (27 Aug. 1932), 156; *Hartlepool Northern Daily Mail*, 28 April 1926.

84 Thomas Burke, *Out and About; a note-book of London in war-time* (1919), 61.

85 *WG*, 27 Aug. 1937; *Birmingham Daily Gazette*, 30 Dec. 1939.

86 *The Sunday Post*, 20 April 1941 & 22 Feb. 1942.

87 *Sussex Express*, 9 Jan. 1942.

88 *Birmingham Daily Post*, 6 March 1941; *Daily Record*, 23 Sept. 1940; *Sunday Pictorial*, 4 Jan. 1942; *NDJ*, 9 Aug. 1945.

89 *Marylebone Mercury*, 30 Dec. 1944; *Tribune*, Issue 697 (May 19, 1950), 2.

90 The programme was broadcast on 17 July 2017: *Irish Times*, 7 June 2019; Margaret Duffy, *Tainted Ground* (2006).

91 J. F. Chanter, 'Uncle Tom Cobley', *DCNQ*, 1911, 7-8.

92 *WT*, 15 Jan. 1909. A typescript letter of 19 July 1902 from Samuel Roach, 'oldest descendant of his living', was placed in Baring-Gould's personal mss copy of the songs: DHC, 5203, no reference number.

93 Brown, 'Some Notes', 167.

94 *EFP*, 3 Jan. 1828; *WT*, 9 Oct. 1841 & 17 Dec. 1842; *EFP*, 18 Jan. 1842. 'He died January 5, at his residence, Butsford, near Colebrooke, aged 82. Thomas Cobley, Esquire., for many years a respected yeoman. His remains were followed to the family vault at Spreyton by a numerous circle of relatives and friends who were all anxious to pay the last tribute of respect to so worthy a man'.

95 Frederic Wordsworth Haydon (ed.), *Benjamin Robert Haydon: Correspondence and Table-Talk* (1876), 429-30; Paul O'Keeffe, *A genius for failure* (2009), 16-17.

96 *Devon Weekly Times*, 9 Aug. 1867; Widecombe & District Local History Group, *History*, 30.

97 C. 'Uncle Tom Cobley', J. S. Attwood, 'Uncle Tom Cobley', *DCNQ*, XI, (Jan. 1920 – Oct. 1921), 70 & J. F. Chanter, 'Uncle Tom Cobley', *DCNQ*, XI, (Jan. 1920 – Oct. 1921), 164; *WT*, 19 May 1939.

98 *Berkshire Chronicle*, 27 Dec. 1902 & 22 April 1905.

99 *WT*, 28 June 1870; *EPG*, 23 April 1891; *WMN*, 26 March 1929; *Shepton Mallet Journal*, 29 March 1929.

100 *Pearson's Weekly*, 6 Aug. 1912; *EPG*, 27 April 1925.

101 Widecombe & District Local History Group, *History*, 84-5; Beatrice Chase, *Dartmoor the Beloved*, 82.

102 *Western Chronicle*, 21 Oct. 1892; *WG*, 10 April 1931; *EPG*, 29 March 1935.

103 *Hull Daily Mail,* 29 Feb., 13 March, 8, 10, 18 & 30 May, 20 June, 22 & 24 July, 12, 13, 21 & 23 Aug. 1940, 19 Sept. 1945, 25 May 1949, 28 Nov. 1939.

104 Colin Chambers, *The Story of Unity Theatre* (New York, 1989), 329; *The Times,* 20 July 1953 & 9 May 1955.

105 *WT,* 3 March 1950; *EFP,* 21 Jan. 1819; *WT,* 14 Sept. 1866; *WMN,* 28 June 1929.

106 *WT,* 22 Jan. 1926.

107 Morton, *In Search,* 113.

108 *EPG,* 8 Feb. 1902 & 11 March 1904; DHC, 6138B; *Daily Mail,* 15 Dec. 1932. For Esso, see *The Economist,* 7 Jan. 1967, vol. 222, Issue 6437, 11.

109 *WT,* 1 June 1934; *Wiltshire Times,* 24 Aug. 1935.

110 *Bucks Examiner,* 30 Aug. 1935.

111 *Nelson Leader,* 29 Nov. 1946.

112 Widecombe & District Local History Group, *History,* 92; www.legendarydartmoor, accessed 28 March 2016. The chair was moved to The Smithy in 2013 from The Old Forge Gift Shop which had had it since the 1990s. The owner's father-in-law's grandfather had purchased it in the 1930s at Cobley's old farm. It was later on view in the Glebe House.

113 DHC, 5215B-O/P/354.

114 *WT,* 25 May 1861; *EFP,* 3 June 1863.

115 *History, Gazetteer & Directory of Devon,* 1878–9, 450.

116 This may have been Henry Toogood of Cheriton Hill: *History, Gazetteer & Directory of Devon, 1878-9,* 450.

117 Baring-Gould, *Further,* 184.

118 R. N. Worth, *The West Country Garland* (1875); Graebe, *As I Walked,* 61-71; Baring Gould, *Songs of the West,* vii; Brown, 'Some Notes', 163; *The Western Antiquary* (July 1888 – June 1889), VIII, v-vii.

119 *WMN,* 10 Oct. 1884; Gray, *Not One of Us,* 93; *EFP,* 24 Sept. 1857; Todd Gray, *Strumpets & Ninnycocks; Name-calling in Devon, 1540–1640* (Exeter, 2016), 47.

120 *NDJ,* 9 Aug. 1832; *Royal Devonport Telegraph,* 4 & 11 Aug. 1832; *Plymouth & Devonport Weekly,* 9 & 16 Aug. 1832. Similar Plymouth ballads were printed in 1801 and 1805: PWDRO, 1/362/37 & 10/1.

121 *EPG,* 29 March 1828; *Taunton Courier,* 2 April 1828; *NDJ,* 3 April 1828.

122 *WT,* 3 Sept. 1842.

123 *WT,* 25 Jan. 1862.

124 *Sidmouth Journal and Directory,* 1 March 1868.

125 *WT,* 21 July 1838; *EPG,* 14 March 1835; *NDJ,* 26 Feb. 1852.

126 *Torquay Times,* 19 Nov. 1870; *WT,* 19 July 1856; *EFP,* 17 July 1856.

127 Baring-Gould, *Further,* 185.

128 Baring-Gould, *Further,* 189; *WDM,* 29 April 1863; *Tavistock Gazette,* 4 Aug. 1882.

129 Graebe, *As I Walked,* 398, 121-5.

130 *WT*, 8 Aug. 1879.

131 Graebe, *As I Walked*, 78-9; Baring-Gould, *Further*, 204.

132 Baring-Gould, *Further*, 199; Graebe, *As I Walked*, 117-119.

133 Baring-Gould, *Further*, 189-91.

134 Baring-Gould, *Further*, 189.

135 Baring-Gould, *Further*, 190.

136 The recording was produced by HMV.

137 TWT, 9 Feb. 1889; *South London Press*, 11 Feb. 1888 & 26 Jan. 1889; *Tewkesbury Register*, 13 Nov. 1875.

138 *WT*, 30 April 1878; *TWT*, 9 Feb. 1889; *Dartmouth Chronicle and Brixham Advertiser*, 15 Dec. 1871; *WMN*, 1 Feb. 1865.

139 *Hastings & St Leonard's Observer*, 14 March 1874.

140 *South London Press*, 24 Jan. 1885; *Sherborne Mercury*, 14 Dec. 1852.

141 *West Sussex County Times*, 21 March 1885; *Daily Reporter*, 23 Sept. 1885; *Buckinghamshire Advertiser*, 14 Feb. 1880, 21 Jan. 1882, 27 Jan. 1883, 22 Sept. 1883, 15 May 1886; *Ipswich Journal*, 17 Feb. 1885; *West Sussex County Times*, 21 March 1885; *Northampton Chronicle*, 23 Sept. 1885.

142 *Hampshire Chronicle*, 30 April 1898; *Taunton Courier*, 28 Nov. 1894; *Sussex Agricultural Express*, 4 March 1892; *Gloucester Citizen*, 1 March 1897; *Chard & Ilminster News*, 27 Oct. 1894; *Bicester Herald*, 19 Feb. 1892.

143 *Manchester Guardian*, 12 Feb. 1895.

144 *Reading Mercury*, 4 Feb. 1899; *Cornish Telegraph*, 10 Nov. 1898; *Cornish & Devon Post*, 21 Dec. 1889; *Bolton Evening News*, 22 Nov. 1909; *Leamington Spa Courier*, 3 Dec. 1898.

145 *Surrey Mirror*, 19 April 1901; *Eastbourne Gazette*, 5 Feb. 1902; *Worcestershire Chronicle*, 27 Dec. 1902.

146 Cecil Sharp & C. L. Marson, *Folk Songs from Somerset* (1911), vol. 2, 48-9.

147 Frederic Thomas Elworthy, *An Outline of the grammar of the dialect of West Somerset* (1877), 82.

148 British Library, C604 & MS Mus. 17771/3/100.

149 *WMN*, 27 Sept. 1888; *The Cornishman and Cornish Telegraph*, 1 Aug. 1929; Dunstan, *Cornish Song Book*, 53; 'Helston Fair', 44; Brown, 'Some Notes', 165; Reeves, *Everlasting Circle*, 164.

150 *Royal Cornwall Gazette*, 16 Jan. 1890; E. K. Chambers, *The English Folk Play* (Oxford, 1933), 62; *Times Telescope for 1831* (1831); Robert Hunt, *Popular romances of the west of England or the drolls, traditions and superstitions of Old Cornwall* (1865), 181; *Sharpe's London Magazine* (1 Nov. 1845), no. 1, 154.

151 'Helston Fair', *Old Cornwall* (Summer, 1934), Vol. 2, Issue 7, 44; Brown, 'Some Notes', 165.

152 *Cornish Telegraph*, 13 Nov. 1913.

153 Ralph Dunstan, *The Cornish Song Book* (1929), 5; *WMN*, 25 Nov. 1891.

154 Brown, 'Some Notes', 165; DHC, 5203, Baring-Gould Personal Copy, *Songs and Ballads of the West*, I, 48.

155 These can be found in Part Three.

156 North American versions have been collected in the mid to late twentieth century in West Virginia ('Joe Maybe, Joe Maybe'), Rhode Island ('Widdecombe Fair') and Ontario ('The Old Country Fair'): VWML, Roud Folksong Index S210566, S273685, S156419. I am grateful to Martin Grabe for drawing my attention to these variants.

157 Sarah Hewett, *The Peasant Speech of Devon* (1892), 139-40. See also K. C. Phillips, *Westcountry Words and Ways* (Newton Abbot, 1976), 24-5.

158 F. T. Elworthy, 'Eighteenth report of the committee on Devonshire verbal provincialisms', *DAT* (1900), XXXII, 59.

159 Baring-Gould, *Songs & Ballads of the West*, Part IV, notes.

160 *WMN*, 12 Sept. 1934; *EPG*, 14 Sept. 1934.

161 Brown, 'Some Notes', 164.

162 *Dartington Hall News*, 2638, 8 April 1971; *Wiltshire Times & Trowbridge Advertiser*, 16 Oct. 1880; *Western Chronicle*, 10 Nov. 1898; *WMN*, 27 Sept. 1888.

163 *The Cornishman and Cornish Telegraph*, 1 Aug. 1929; Dunstan, *Cornish Song Book*, 53; 'Helston Fair', 44; Brown, 'Some Notes', 165; Reeves, *Everlasting Circle*, 164.

164 *WT*, 28 Sept. 1934.

165 Widecombe & District Local History Group, *History*, 28-30; Baring-Gould, *Songs of the West*, notes on the songs, 6.

166 Widecombe & District Local History Group, *History*, 1, 5.

167 Joseph Wright, *The English Dialect Dictionary* (Oxford, 1905), Vol. 3, 222; A. G. Collings, 'Devon's Woodcock Field-Names', *DCNQ* (Spring, 2019), XLII, Pt V, 158.

168 J. F. Chanter, 'Uncle Tom Cobley', *Devonian Year Book* (1920), 67 & *DCNQ* (1921), XI, 7.

169 *WMN*, 26 Sept. 1888.

170 *WMN*, 27 Sept. 1888.

171 Plymouth & West Devon Record Office, 3180 & 1984, reproduced in Martin Graebe & Ian Maxted, *Songs of the West; Baring-Gould Heritage Project* (Exeter, 1998); Brown, 'Some Notes', 164.

172 J. A. Fuller Maitland, 'Report of the second meeting of the folk-song society', *Journal of the Folk-Song Society*, Vol. 1, No. 2 (1900), 30; VWML, Lucy Broadwood Mss, LEB/4/233.

173 *EPG*, 2 Dec. 1932.

174 *The Cornishman and Cornish Telegraph*, 1 Aug. 1929; Dunstan, *Cornish Song Book*, 53; 'Helston Fair', 44; Brown, 'Some Notes', 165; James Reeves, *Everlasting Circle* (1960), 164.

175 Fred Hamer, *Garner's Gay* (1967), 10-11; VWML, H. H. Albino Collection; *Gloucestershire Echo*, 11 March 1936; Reeves, *Everlasting Circle*, 164; Maud Karpeles, *Cecil Sharp's Collection of English Folk Songs* (Oxford, 1974), II, 365-6; *Kinrosss-shire Advertiser*, 8 Feb. 1908; *Sussex Express*, 8 May 1931.

176 James Orchard Halliwell, *Nursery Rhymes of England* (1886), 301.

177 See the Appendices.

178 R. J. Yeatman, *Horse Nonsense* (1933), 118-119.

179 Ken Dodd and the Diddymen (1968).

180 *Worker's Liberty* (April 1997); *Personal Computer News* (18 March 1983), *Doctor Who Magazine* (Sept. 2008), *Sports Illustrated* (15 Nov. 1954), *Fortean Times* (Feb. 2015); *Practical Wireless* (Feb. 1967); *Australian Women's Weekly* (22 Jan. 1938); *Radio Communication* (Feb. 1990); *National Geographic* (July 1963); *The Hollywood Reporter* (Jan. – June 1934); *The Entomologist's Record* (1978); *Motion Picture Exhibitor* (3 April 1963); *Flight International Magazine* (29 June 1922); *Smash Hits* (3 May 1979); *The Chemist & Druggist* (21 Oct. 1961); *The Jerusalem Post Magazine* (1 April 1977).

181 *EFP*, 6 Oct. 1825; W. F. Collier, 'Some sixty years' reminiscences of Plymouth', *DAT* (1892), XXIV, 89; W. F. Collier, 'Devonshire Dialect', *DAT* (1893), XXV, 276-85; William Collier, 'Portrait of a young Quaker', *DAT* (1996), CXXVIII, 101, 106; Elizabeth Crawford, *The Women's Suffrage Movement in Britain and Ireland* (Abingdon, 2006), 153; Graebe, *As I Walked*, 68, 121, 303. He died at Woodtown on 9 Feb. 1902: *Globe*, 12 Feb. 1902; *WMN*, 19 Feb. 1902; William Frederick Collier, *Tales and Sayings of William Robert Hicks of Bodmin* (Truro, 1903), 18-25.

182 It was published in sections with the first two appearing in 1889: *Morning Post*, 22 Nov. 1889; S. Baring-Gould & H. Fleetwood Sheppard, *Songs and Ballads of the West* (1889), Part I, xvii.

183 DHC, 5203, no reference number; S. Baring Gould, H. Fleetwood Sheppard & F. W. Bussell, *Songs of the West* (1905 edn), No. 16.

184 Oswald J. Reichel, 'Songs of the West', *Devon Notes & Queries* (1907), IV, 56.

185 DHC, 5203, Baring-Gould Personal Copy, *Songs and Ballads of the West*, I, 48.

186 Douglas Gordon, 'Uncle Tom Cobley and all', *Country Life*, Vol. 90, issue 2321, 12 July 1941, 62-3.

187 *WMN*, 15 March 1940 & 23 Sept. 1938; Anthony Greenstreet, 'Douglas St Leger-Gordon', *Dartmoor Magazine*, 76 (2004), 12-13.

188 Douglas Gordon, *Dartmoor In All Its Moods* (1931), p127.

189 Census, Belstone, 1891.

190 BL, C604/10.

191 *Dartington Hall News*, 2638, 8 April 1971.

192 Census, Belstone, 1891.

193 *WMN*, 27 Sept. 1888. He lived at Langley Terrace.

194 *WMN*, 26 Sept. 1888 & 9 May 1895.

195 This information was derived from the censuses of those years.

196 *WMN*, 28 Sept. 1888. Baring-Gould's manuscript notes from the article's verses have transcription errors.

197 *The Musical Times*, Vol. 20, Issue 432, Feb. 1897, 100; *Torquay Times*, 15 Feb. 1895 & 21 Dec. 1888, 11 Nov. 1904.

198 Marjory Eckett Fielden, 'Living Memories in Devon', *DAT* (1935), LXVII, 387-8; *Torquay Times*, 30 Dec. 1892.

199 *WT*, 22 Jan. 1889; *TWT*, 26 Jan. 1889; *Sporting Times*, 28 Feb. 1903.

200 For instance, W. Davies, 'Notes on Kingsbridge Documents, etc.', *DAT* (1901), XXXIII, 651-6.

201 *Sporting Times*, 17 Jan. 1903.

202 'Voices From the Past', Colebrooke Bell (Colebrooke, 2019), Mabel Lee, 1901-1998. I am grateful to Carole Herbert for this reference.

203 *Sporting Times*, 31 Jan. 1903.

204 *WT*, 27 Dec. 1912.

205 He married in 1916, thirteen years after he recorded the ballad: *Ealing Gazette*, 1 July 1916.

206 *The Guardian*, 29 June 2006; *Dartington Hall News*, 2638, 8 April 1971; British Library, C604 & MS Mus. 17771/3/100.

207 Information supplied by Stanley Oldfield.

208 Census, Harberton, 1911; *WT*, 10 Jan. 1941; *EPG*, 28 Jan. 1949 & 9 June 1950; *WT*, 7 July 1950.

209 *WMN*, 23 Sept. 1948; British Library, C604 & MS Mus. 17771/3/100.

210 *Devon Weekly Times*, 9 Aug. 1867; *EPG*, 13 Feb. 1880.

211 Charles H. Laycock, 'English national and folk music, with special reference to the folk-songs of Devonshire', *DAT* (1917), XLIX, 316; J. F. Chanter, 'Uncle Tom Cobley', *The Devonian Year Book* (1920), 67 & *DCNQ* (1921), XI, 7.

212 *WMN*, 26 Sept. 1888.

213 *EPG*, 13 Feb. 1880; George P. R. Pulman, *The Song of Solomon in the East Devonshire Dialect* (1860); W. R. Wilkin, 'Some Axminster Worthies (Part II)', *DAT* (1934), LXVI, 240-44; *Southern Times & Dorset County Herald*, 14 Feb. 1880; EFP, 1 Dec. 1859.

214 Charles H. Farnsworth & Cecil J. Sharp (eds), *Folk-songs, chanteys and singing games* (New York, 1916), 1-5. It was republished in *Song Ballads and Other Songs of the Pine Mountain Settlement School* (1923), 35-6.

215 *New York Times*, 23 May 1947.

216 *Taunton Courier & Western Advertiser*, 9 Oct. 1937.

217 *WT*, 28 Sept. 1934; *EPG*, 18 Oct. 1935.

218 VWML, Lucy Broadwood Mss, LEB/4/233.

219 *WT*, 30 April 1878.

220 *NDJ*, 3 Nov. 1904.

221 *WDM*, 27 Aug. & 18 Nov. 1920.

222 VWML, Lucy Broadwood MSS, LEB/4/230.

223 *Taunton Courier & Western Advertiser*, 9 Oct. 1937; Sharp & Marson, *Folk Songs From Somerset*, II, 48-9.

224 Sharp & Marson, *Folk Songs*, II, 48-9; *West Somerset Free Press*, 18 Nov. 1905; VWLM,

Cecil Sharp MSS, Folk Words, 412-3; W. G. NcNaught, *Novello's School Songs* (1908), Midsummer Fair; Karpeles, *Cecil Sharp's Collection*, 365-6.

225 *Central Somerset Gazette*, 12 Oct. 1923.

226 Karpeles, *Cecil Sharp's Collection*, 366.

227 Karpeles, *Cecil Sharp's Collection*, 627.

228 VWLM, Plunkett Collection (Sussex texts transcript).

229 VWML, Roud Bib. X8644; BL, Sound Recordings, Lansdown Fair (Tom Pearce), C903/196; University of Sheffield, Special Collections, Russell Wortley Collection, notebook; Kenndy, *Folksongs*, 682.

230 *The Children's Newspaper*, 7 Feb. 1953; *The Times*, 17 & 26 Jan. 1953.

231 VWML, H. H. Albino Mss Collection, Folder 40, Field Notebook 1, 30-3. See also Folder 7.

232 VWML, JHB, volumes 2, 3 & 7; Peter Kennedy (ed.), *Folksongs of Britain and Ireland* (1975), 682.

233 Brown, 'Some Notes', 165; 'Helston Fair', 44; *Western Morning News*, 21 Jan. 1936.

234 Reeves, *Everlasting Circle*, 164.

235 VWML, GG/1/1067; *Kinross-shire Advertiser*, 5 Feb. 1908.

236 *Kinross-shire Advertiser*, 5 Feb. 1908.

237 Hamer, *Garner's Gay*, 10.

238 Ruth Harvey and Miss Gilchrist, 'Two Folk Songs', *Journal of the English Folk Dance and Song Society*, Vol. 4, No. 2 (Dec. 1941), 77-8.

239 Thomas Wood, 'Folk Songs from the Essex-Suffolk Border', *Journal of the Folk Song Society*, Vol. 8, No. 33 (Dec. 1929), 132-3.

240 Ruth Harvey and Miss Gilchrist, 'Two Folk Songs', 77-8.

241 *Tait's Magazine* (1843), X, 121.

242 James Orchard Halliwell, *Popular Rhymes and Nursery Tales* (1849), 272-4.

243 L. Edna Walter, *Mother Goose's Nursery Rhymes* (1919), 130-1.

244 *Dartington Hall News*, 2638, 1971.

245 *The Devonian Year Book* (1915), 20; *The Globe*, 15 Dec. 1914.

246 *WT*, 15 Jan. 1915 & 3 March 1916; *The Cornishman*, 4 Nov. 1915. The London version was noted as having been written by Bill Adams.

247 The recording was made by HMV.

248 *Buckingham Advertiser*, 4 March 1916.

249 Imperial War Museum, ts, 1 July 1915, from *Home Chat: South Atlantic Leader*, pages 7-8, on ProQuest Wellesley index to Victorian periodicals.

250 *Hartlepool Northern Daily Mail*, 4 Aug. 1936.

251 *Yorkshire Evening Post*, 24 Jan. 1940.

252 *The Sketch*, 8 Oct. 1941.

253 *Yorkshire Evening Post*, 21 March 1952; *Tormorden & District News*, 17 June 1932.

254 *Forfar Dispatch*, 26 April 1945.

255 *NDJ*, 13 & 20 Sept. 1934.

256 *WMN*, 17 June 1909.

257 *Portsmouth Evening News*, 20 July 1932; *Belfast News-Letter*, 29 June 1932; *Hull Daily Mail*, 4 July 1932; *Nottingham Evening Post*, 17 June 1932; *The Sphere*, 14 March 1931.

258 *Tatler*, 9 April, 1947; *Illustrated London News*, 5 July 1947; *The Sphere*, 9 Aug. 1947.

259 DHC, LE 1761/EG2 (Exeter Garland), https://bookhistory.blogspot.com/2015/01/election-ephemera-devon.html 'Devon election ephemera: Ide burlesque election'.

260 *Dartmouth & South Hams Chronicle*, 1 Dec. 1869.

261 National Archives, MH 13/60/121.

262 Sabine Baring-Gould, *A Collection of Ballads* (1924), I, 287-8.

263 *Devon & Exeter Daily Gazette*, 6 & 8 June 1894.

264 *Exmouth Journal*, 2, 9 & 23 June, 21 & 28 July, 18 & 25 Aug., 29 Sept. 1894, & 15 May 1897.

265 *EPG*, 22 Oct. 1909.

266 *Liverpool Daily Post & Mercury*, 6 Dec. 1906; *The Sphere*, 19 Jan. 1907.

267 *Willesden Chronicle* and *The Kilburn Times*, 18 Nov. 1904.

268 *WMN*, 22 Jan. 1910.

269 *WT*, 19 Jan. 1906.

270 *South Bucks Standard*, 11 March 1910.

271 *NDJ*, 20 Jan. 1910.

272 Laura Beers, *Red Ellen* (Cambridge, Mass., 2016), 107-9; Pat Francis, 'The Labour Publishing Company 1920-9', *History Workshop*, No. 18 (Autumn, 1984), 116-117.

273 University of Sussex Special Collections, GB 181 SxMs 44; Maurice Reckitt, *As It Happened* (1941), 79, 82-3, 202; G. D. H. & Margaret Cole, *The Bolo Book* (1921), 40-1.

274 *The Communist Solar System* (1956), 59.

275 *Hendon & Finchley Times*, 6 Oct. 1922 & 25 Aug. 1939.

276 *Hendon & Finchley Times*, 20 Nov. 1925.

277 *Hendon & Finchley Times*, 26 June 1936.

278 *Bedfordshire Times & Independent*, 6 July 1951.

279 Philip Thornton, *The Voice of Atlas* (1936), 221-2.

280 Leonardo Castellani, *Camperas* (2006 edn), 15-16; Alberto Ciria, *Parties and Power in Modern Argentina*, 1930-46 (Albany, 1974), 125.

281 Percy C. Buck (ed.), *The Oxford Song Book* (Oxford, 1921), 202.

282 Félix Rose, *Les Grands Lyriques Anglais* (Paris, 1940), 387 & 389.

283 *Times Literary Supplement*, Issue 1996, 4 May 1940, 213; *Surrey Mirror*, 31 March 1944.

284 Deborah Devonshire, *Counting My Chickens* (Ebrington, 2001), 157-8; Adam Sisman (ed.), *The Letters of Patrick Leigh Fermor* (2016), letter of 1 Feb. 1960; Patrick Leigh Fermor, memorial order of service, Church of St James, Piccadilly, 15 Dec. 2011.

285 *South Polar Times* (August 1903), 44-5; Caroline Philpott and Elizabeth Leane, 'Making Music on the March: Sledging Songs of the Heroic Age of Antarctic Exploration', *Polar Record* (Nov. 2016), Vol. 52, Issue 6, 698-716.

286 *WMN*, 26 Sept. 1921; Margaret & James Fisher, *Shackleton and the Antarctic* (Cambridge, 1957), 345.

287 John Hirst, *The Songs of the Mountaineers* (Manchester, c1922), 60; *Penrith Observer*, 28 Aug. 1928.

288 *Buckingham Advertiser and North Bucks Free Press*, 15 Jan. 1927.

289 *Punch*, CCXVII, No. 5692, 28 Dec. 1949, 714.

290 *Irish Independent*, 20 June 1950.

291 John Rylands Library, GB 133 ERS, diaries volume one, 8 March 1933; Marguerite Dupree (ed.), *Lancashire and Whitehall, the diary of Sir Raymond Street* (Manchester, 1987), I, 218.; Greater Manchester County Record Office, b10/10/3/3726/1; *The Engineer*, 20 Nov. 1959.

292 *Leeds Mercury*, 11 Jan. 1933; *Lancashire Evening Post*, 14 Feb. 1933; Dupree, *Lancashire and Whitehall*, introduction.

293 *Black & White*, Vol. XIX, No. 49 (23 June 1900).

294 It was broadcast in the third series on 12 February 1967 as part of 'The Plastic Max'; Christopher Stevens, *Kenneth Williams: Born Brilliant: The Life of Kenneth Wililams*, no page numbers.

295 Kenneth Wiliams, *Rambling Syd Rumpo in Concert* (Parlophone, 1967); Martin Dibbs, *Radio Fun and the BBC Variety Department, 1922-67* (Cham, 2019), 264.

Index

Use of bold indicates illustrations